GROWING BEANS

A DIET FOR HEALTHY
PEOPLE AND PLANET

SUSAN YOUNG

Permanent Publications

Published by
Permanent Publications
Hyden House Ltd
The Sustainability Centre
East Meon
Hampshire
GU32 1HR
United Kingdom
Tel: 01730 776 582
        International: +44 (0)1730 776 582
Email: enquiries@permaculture.co.uk
Web: www.permanentpublications.co.uk

Distributed in North America by
Chelsea Green Publishing Company, PO Box 428, White River Junction, VT 05001, USA
www.chelseagreen.com

Designed by Two Plus George Limited, info@twoplusgeorge.co.uk

Cover photographs by Gail Harland

Photographs by Susan Young, Brian Wiltshire and Gail Harland

Printed in the UK by Bell & Bain, Thornliebank, Glasgow

All paper from FSC certified mixed sources
The Forest Stewardship Council (FSC) is a non-profit
international organisation established to promote the
responsible management of the world's forests. Products
carrying the FSC label are independently certified to assure
consumers that they come from forests that are managed to
meet the social, economic and ecological needs of present
and future generations.

British Library Cataloguing-in-Publication Data
A catalogue record for this book is available from the British Library

ISBN 978 1 85623 218 0

TESTIMONIALS

This great new book should ensure that the humble dried bean finally gets the boost it deserves to make it a must-grow veg on every UK allotment. Packed with amazing facts on the long history of the crop, it also offers all the advice you'll ever need to help you sow, grow, harvest, store and cook it. A fascinating book – I guarantee having read it you'll want to add this neglected superfood to your annual list of sowing essentials.

Steve Ott
editor of *Kitchen Garden Magazine*

Legumes such as beans, lentils, peas and peanuts have always been a staple of my diet, in harmony with whole grains and vegetables. That same harmony works in the field, where beans help to maintain soil health and fertility. Susan Young has given beans the prominence they deserve – anyone who reads her book will have a much greater appreciation of the value of beans in our diet and in agriculture.

Craig Sams
founder of Carbon Gold Biochar and Green & Black's chocolate, and former chair of the Soil Association

Growing Beans is an inspiring, mouth-watering and practical guide to growing beans and much more. Susan Young's personal love of beans is infectious and she persuasively sets out why we all should all be growing and eating more beans, for our own and the planet's sake. It's full of fascinating history, charming wit and sensible easy-to-follow advice on choosing, growing, storing and cooking beans. We love this book as much as we love beans!

Nick Saltmarsh
Managing Director, Hodmedod Ltd, https://hodmedods.co.uk

Growing Beans provides the reader with a comprehensive and interesting read, highlighting one of Nature's 'wonder' crops. Susan covers everything from their unrivalled health benefits to us, their ability to sequester carbon and their eco credentials, to even where and how we can grow and consume them ourselves. I found the book a must read for anyone wanting to discover more about growing beans.

James Maguire-Dunckel
President, Pulses UK, www.pulsesuk.co.uk

Shifting perceptions of the humble bean is quite a task given their blemished history. Young makes this challenge an opportunity and an excitement for British gardeners. A much welcomed book encouraging the love of growing and eating the world's most climate-friendly food.

Amelia Christie-Miller
Bold Bean Co, https://boldbeanco.com

As growers, gardeners and cooks we tend to relegate the bean to the back of the garden or the store cupboard, so it is wonderful to read Susan Young's book and really take inspiration from her obvious passion for the bean. And of course what is not to love? Whatever your dietary choice, beans are a great way to bring homegrown protein into any diet whilst also giving people the option to grow their own, even in a large container, so not relying on a huge amount of space. Plus the pollinators love the flowers, so let's get planting!

Sara Venn
Edible Bristol, https://ediblebristol.org.uk

The climate emergency is forcing us to rethink global methods of food production and farming systems. It is clear that we need to move away from animal-based industrialised agriculture in favour of small farm futures and locally-based diet solutions. Beans and legumes, currently undervalued as sources of protein for human beings, will play a much larger role in any future diet for our small planet, and Susan Young here provides a comprehensive, practical and fun guide to their cultivation, history and many, many uses.

Graham Burnett
permaculture teacher and author of *Vegan Book of Permaculture*

What a timely book; with so many of us turning to more sustainable ways of living, what could be better than a guide to growing one of the most delicious and beneficial crops on the planet? From the nutritional and environmental pluses of eating beans, to the practicalities of sourcing seeds, nurturing plants, storing and cooking, Susan gives a wonderfully engaging and informative guide for any keen gardener-cook.

Jenny Chandler
author of *Pulse* and *Green Kids Cook*, www.jennychandlerblog.com

Beans are the foundation for wonderful staple and delicious dishes across so many cultures. This book is a great guide and shows us how to grow beans easily and sustainably, and to eating healthily and well. There's so much to enjoy, learn and try here.

Kalpna Woolf
91 Ways Founder, https://91ways.org

ACKNOWLEDGEMENTS

Brian Wiltshire took many of the photos; the best ones are his.

John Hunter expertly filmed beans growing in my garden as I talked about them.

Matt Dunn and Freyja Sears of One Planet Smallholding grew beans for me to trial when I had run out of space in my own garden.

Patrick Kaiser of Tatgut in Germany generously sent bean varieties for free with encouraging messages of information and support.

Maddy Harland, Rozie Apps, Gail Harland and the team at Permanent Publications were positive about the book when I first suggested it to them and were always helpful, well organised and so easy to work with.

And finally to Michael, who has patiently listened to me talking about beans, has cooked and eaten a lot of beans, and was enthusiastic about 'the bean book' from the start.

ABOUT THE AUTHOR

Retirement from a career of teaching in schools and universities allowed Susan Young to devote more time to gardening, and growing vegetables. She has lived for the last 20 years on two acres in the Wye Valley, on the English-Welsh border, part of which she gardens and the rest maintains as a wildflower meadow. But it was the pandemic and lockdown, a time to reassess and reconnect, that prompted her to write a book based on a passion for searching out and growing beans.

Originally trained as a pianist she has spent many years as a music educator and university lecturer, with degrees in music, education and biological anthropology. She has written many books and articles about music education. From writing about education to writing about growing beans may seem to be a wide leap, but there is a connecting thread, one of hoping to motivate change for the better – whether it's for improved education, care for the environment or healthy lifestyles.

For my grandchildren – Alice and Harry, Charlie and Ted

CONTENTS

PREFACE

Growing towards a better future

Mentioning beans may bring to mind the canned Beanz variety, rude rhymes or penny-pinching diets. But beans belong to that vast legume family of edible seeds that are one of our most nutritious, concentrated and durable foods – and also one of the most underrated and neglected, certainly as a garden crop. They are easy to grow, easy to cook, nourishing, healthy for us and the planet – and most important of all, they taste good. Very good indeed.

Beans are an ancient food that has nourished a host of past civilizations and remain a staple food in many parts of the world, yet for some reason, many of us have yet to discover the delights of beans in all their variety and deliciousness. Why don't we grow and eat more?

I think the answer is simple. We don't have a long-standing tradition of growing beans in our gardens and allotments to the shelling and drying stage to appreciate their qualities and the seeds are not readily avail]able in seed catalogues. Our culinary tradition does not include dishes that cook beans to bring out their best and prompt us to want to grow what we want to eat.

This book aims to change all that.

chapter 1

Why we should grow and eat beans

The family of pulses includes peas, lentils and beans, but it is beans, or more precisely beans eaten at the shelling stage or dried to eat later, that this book is all about. Although the word bean is applied loosely to everything from broad beans to soya, I focus on the family of beans (*Phaseolus*) that includes all those that we might also call haricot, kidney, navy, flageolet and the big fat beans that runner bean plants produce.

Fixing food has never been more important. In 2020-21, the year of the pandemic, an important global platform calling for food system transformation named EAT stated that shifting diets could unlock climate, health, environmental benefits and reduce the risk of future pandemics. Replacing overconsumption of meat by eating more vegetables, grains, nuts and pulses is key to changing our diets. Beans have a crucial role to play in replacing animal proteins that are costly to produce and are a drain on the earth's resources. As gardeners, we can grow them, and lots of them.

Vegetable growing traditions among gardeners are led by what we like to eat. Or perhaps it is better to say that there is a process of co-evolution between growing and cooking traditions. Eating habits in Britain don't currently include a lot of beans, well, except for the tinned Beanz variety of course. Meat and two veg – potatoes and the usual range of root and leaf vegetables – have remained the staples of vegetable eating. These staples have dictated what commercial seed sellers offer and what gardeners tend to grow. Pulses are grown as peas and broad beans, but bean growing is typically limited to producing beans to eat at the green stage and not at the shelling or dried stage. Dried beans have long been seen as only good for throwing into stews or soups where everything but the bean adds the flavour. Usually these beans are the staple varieties, a red kidney bean or plain haricot, bought ready-packaged, dry, hard and ordinary. But beans are finally, gradually being recognised and celebrated in their own right, for their individual, delicious flavours, textures and appearance. They are delectable on their own, with only the lightest of flavourings, or can be the main ingredient in the most wonderful range of endlessly variable dishes.

Although our British cuisine has not evolved over the years to include beans, luckily we don't have to look far from home to find food cultures and growing traditions from which we can learn. Across Europe from Sweden to Greece, Portugal to Bulgaria, bean cultivation has flourished in the hands of gardeners and small-scale farmers who have grown them for their own consumption or to sell locally. Cooking traditions based on locally grown beans have evolved with far greater versatility and variety than our British cooking habits. At the same time, Britain is home to a wide diversity of communities who have brought with them culinary traditions from Asia, Africa and the Caribbean that include delicious pulse dishes.

So in this book I hope to convince you to make some changes to what you grow to eat – the why to grow and eat beans, as well as the how.

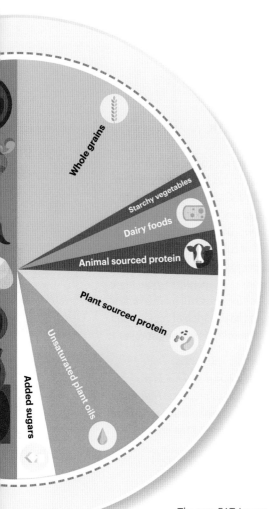

Whole grains

Starchy vegetables

Dairy foods

Animal sourced protein

Plant sourced protein

Unsaturated plant oils

Added sugars

The 2019 EAT-Lancet Commission report modelled a healthy diet for the world that could be produced without damaging ecosystems. It estimated the need to double fruit and vegetable productions worldwide. The planetary health diet emphasises a plant-forward diet where whole grains, fruits, vegetables, nuts and legumes comprise a greater proportion of foods consumed. Meat and dairy constitute important parts of the diet but in significantly smaller proportions than whole grains, fruits, vegetables, nuts and legumes.

The education of the cook ...

In 1885 William Robinson wrote a preface to the English translation of Vilmorin-Andrieux's famous French compendium of garden vegetables, The Vegetable Garden. *Here he wrote 'a few generations only have passed since our now commonest vegetables came from the Continent. We are adding to their number every day, and by the aid of cultivation we are winning back our way to a simpler, healthier food ... But the education of the cook bars the way to progress ... We ought to grow more kinds of vegetables than we do, but we need still more a radical change in our modes of cookery, in the direction of cooking and serving [of vegetables] for their own sakes (and in most cases without animal substance) ...'*

William Robinson wrote this in 1885, but it still holds true. The education of the cook bars the way to progress. That said, this is a gardening book. But growing, cooking and eating form one continuous cycle, each process influencing the others.

'Mariazeller'

chapter 2

How I came to be enthusiastic about beans

I'm not sure when I first fell in love with beans. Maybe it was the day we discovered a small warehouse full of dried beans down a narrow backstreet in Oaxaca, Mexico. Open sacks covered the floor filled with every size and colour of bean imaginable, carelessly spilling out across the floor. I left clutching several paper bags of different beans bought through gesture alone. Maybe it was sitting in the scented evening air at a Greek taverna eating *gigantes plaki*; a tasty mix of tomatoes, spices, oil and huge white Greek beans. Maybe it was a dish of pale green haricot beans in Italy, dressed with the merest dash of lemon and oil. Maybe it was in Bilbao, northern Spain, as freezing winter rains swept in from the ocean, sitting in a snug backstreet restaurant tucking into an earthenware dish brimming with inky black beans.

The dried bean, or in the form of fresh shelling beans, has none of the trendiness of heirloom tomatoes or oddly shaped fiery chilli peppers. This is a puzzle. Beans ask so little of us as gardeners but give so much in return. There are thousands of beautiful beans that all have distinct flavours and textures. They may grow a foot high or ten feet, produce beans the size of rice grains or gobstoppers, beans of every jewelled colour imaginable, striped, spotted, speckled and splotched. They can be cooked in any number of delicious ways. They are good for you. They are good for the planet.

Many years back in the 1970s, influenced by vegetarian friends, I bought a cookery book called *Diet for a Small Planet*. I still have this book, pages yellowing with age, but its ecological arguments for the use of soil to produce vegetable protein rather than meat protein are even more urgent today than they were then, 50 years ago, as we understand the extreme consequences of global warming and pollution. The argument that *Diet for a Small Planet* sets out is clear, simple and utterly convincing. Society today faces many challenges: global warming, water scarcity, obesity, heart disease, diabetes and many more. In each case, growing and eating pulses can be part of the solution.

Today in the UK we eat fewer pulses than average around the world. Yet canned baked Beanz are eaten in vast quantities, more than 2.5 million cans per day. All the beans used for baked beans are imported. I discovered that around 50,000 tonnes are shipped annually from North America to Liverpool docks and delivered daily to the Heinz factory in Wigan, the largest baked bean factory in the world. These are the uniform navy beans grown in the vast, agro-industrial fields of the US and Canada. Yet beans are grown commercially in Britain in surprisingly large quantities. These are field beans, *Vicia faba* or fava beans. Approximately 740,000 tonnes of fava beans are harvested each year in the UK, mainly used for animal feed or exported. It's a little known fact that the UK is one of the biggest fava bean exporters globally, mainly sending beans to Egypt and Japan. Anyone who has tasted roasted fava beans knows just what we are missing by sending these crops overseas. So the madness is that Britain exports quantities of one type of bean and imports quantities of a different type of bean. I do not need to point out that both imports and exports travel wastefully long distances.

It's only when you start to delve into the world of beans across Europe and North America that you realise there is very little choice of bean seeds available in most UK seed catalogues. The range of varieties intended for shelling out and eating as beans, rather than the pod 'mangetout' style, is extremely limited. The company Seeds of Italy has introduced us to beans from Italy but there is no Seeds of Holland, say, that has shown us the delights of Dutch beans, or further afield into Germany, Poland, Austria and the countries of eastern Europe or reaching down into France, Spain and Portugal.

And it's only when you look at how beans have been used in the cuisines of European countries that it becomes clear that we have no tradition of using beans – shelling or dried beans – to create the wonderful array of delectable dishes that our European friends and

A field of fava beans. © *Hodmedods*

those further afield in the Americas and Asian countries enjoy. There are so many types of beans with textures and flavours ranging from sweet, creamy and delicate to chestnutty, rich and earthy. We are missing out.

Beans have traditionally been the food of the poor. So they carry a marker of class and this could account for some of the continuing bias towards them, and probably accounts for the lack of imagination in British cookery traditions. Yet there is also a reverse turn to humble foods. Peasant food evokes wholesomeness, simple tastes, contact with the soil and rustic roots. And yet, perversely, a bag of authentic, appellation beans from France can command an astronomical price and will be spooned sparingly onto plates in top restaurants. Embracing the common bean, in all its simplicity, carries so many different resonances. But this diversity of resonances is a strength. Different ideas interconnect and reinforce one another. In the present day, concerns about health and the environment are uppermost for many people. The pandemic of 2020 has also prompted us to reassess our values and lifestyles. We have lived at home, been close to our gardens, we have cooked, and grown, and thought again about what matters the most.

I then turned to my collection of vegetable gardening books to look for information about bean growing. There is surprisingly little. Of course there are sections for runner beans and French beans – and occasionally the comment that beans can also be eaten as fresh shelled beans or can be dried – but no serious forays into the wide range of varieties, or the details of how to grow, harvest and dry them. Shelling beans are, it is thought, tricky to bring to a plump bean or on to a dry-able state with our English summers. It is true they need a bit more fussing over than some crops but I have never had difficulty. Even with the wettest of years when I've been slow to plant them out, the beans do okay, although not so abundantly perhaps. But even so, it doesn't take many bean plants of several varieties to produce enough dried beans or frozen shelled beans in the freezer to last two of us through the year.

In the past few years I have tried to be more conscientious about planting early indoors, planting out and tending the bean plants, and noting the weather in relation to their ripening. But they burgeon – they bloom, bulge and burst their pods – much of the time I walk past them in the garden giving them little more than a glance. When I've time, I may walk among them and take a look. I dangle the hose pipe at their roots if they look dryish and feed them every once in a while when they are in flower and the pods are starting to form. But I am a casual and often careless gardener. The beans are not neatly supported, they flop, and fall about. They outgrow their often inadequate climbing supports, weighing them down. But still they produce – willingly, obligingly and abundantly, with pretty white, lilac, red and pink flowers to top it all.

Gardening books are written to give information to gardeners on what they are in the habit of growing. Few gardening books are written to try to change habits of what we grow and why. Gardeners grow vegetables that they want to eat. Our vegetable eating traditions in Britain are conservative – dare I say, dull. So vegetable growing traditions in the UK have stayed very much the same, rarely adventuring beyond the standard peas, cabbages, carrots and runner beans. Borlotti beans may get a mention in some of the more recent vegetable gardening books, but that's usually as far as it goes. Seed catalogues, likewise, list the vegetables that gardeners have always grown and ask for. Admittedly what seed sellers can offer is limited by regulations. So how does change happen?

On the cookery side, there are increasing numbers of books offering recipes for pulses, many catering for the move towards vegetarian and vegan diets. These recipe books draw on the bean cooking traditions from many countries of Europe. In Italy, France and Spain in particular, there are special beans for special regions – a kind of champagne appellation for the very best and most delicious. There are bean cooking traditions in the Middle East, delicately flavoured, and from the Far East, fiery and pungently spiced. And the bean growing and eating traditions of South America and the USA are second to none. Perhaps tinned beans have dulled our palette for the subtleties and enormous varieties of flavours that bean dishes offer. Although I should add that little beats homemade baked beans in tomato sauce; that combination of fresh beans and homegrown tomatoes, basil, thyme and plenty of garlic.

I do not consider myself to be a vegetable growing expert. Just an ordinary competent-enough vegetable grower who has grown vegetables all my life, like almost all who will read this book I imagine. Nor, when I started out with this book, was I much of an expert on beans. Nor am I an expert cook with a flair for vegetarian cookery. But my very inexpertness and the fact that I had to research and explore beans and growing them from scratch is what I offer. My experiments and experiences with certain varieties allow me to recommend them for successful cultivation in our climate.

At the start I bought the handful of books about beans that I could find. These books are from the US and orientated to that food culture, their growing climate and the bean varieties that

'Alubias Negras de Tolosa'

are available and popular in North America. In North America there is a long and proud bean heritage going back to its indigenous populations, to strong connections with South America and the arrival of European immigrants during the pioneering days. British gardeners, on the whole, in part due to early industrialisation, don't have the same connections to heirloom crops. I searched and read, gradually collecting facts and information and piecing it together. And of course, for the few years it has taken to prepare this book I have grown and eaten beans – lots and lots of beans.

This brings me to a delicate matter that needs to be mentioned before we go any further. The wind factor. Well, it's true that beans do cause flatulence, but this is all linked with how many you eat, how accustomed your digestive system is to bean consumption, what varieties you eat and how you prepare them. But let us also remember that the wind is part of what makes them very good for you. The carbohydrate in beans is complex and compound and so takes a long time to digest. For this reason you stay feeling full and satisfied for a long time after a bean meal, unlike simple sugars that slip through leaving you wanting more very soon. The bean provides roughage that helps to keep your gut healthy. There are many more health benefits

Zolfino

and I devote a short chapter to these (see p. 13), having carefully gone through the research and presenting this in straightforward terms.

And growing beans provides a long season crop. The good news is that some varieties of beans can do triple duty as young green bean pods, fresh shelling beans and finally dried beans. But although all French or runner beans can be grown on to the shelling stage, that does not mean that the modern green bean will turn into a good and productive shell or dried bean. They have been bred to be tender as green pods with slow seed development, and the final seeds are slim to reduce the unwanted swelling that thins and toughens the all-important pod. For a shelling bean though, plumpness is what we want and certainly in cooler, northern climates, we need the seed to develop faster and fatter in the pod. Some beans grown for shelling are still good at the green bean stage and many traditional, heritage beans are multi-purpose, offering food for the kitchen over a long period, ideal for the home producer. But some shelling beans, particularly the older varieties, have tough, stringy, thin pods that are not suitable for eating at that stage.

Once you start discovering the enormous variety of beans and how beautiful they are, it is easy to become captivated. There are bean enthusiasts who are so in love with the treasure trove of shapes, colours, patterns and histories of beans that they collect them, hunting down the rare and interesting. I completely understand how it can become compulsive to collect and start swapping with other bean-fanatics. Holding and handling them is a pleasure and for certain these bean collectors are helping to preserve varieties that date back to the 1800s, even earlier perhaps, maintaining gene banks of seeds. These seeds may have disease resistance, or grow better in drought, or have some other advantage that the more modern cultivars have lost. But while I love their beauty and how tactile they are, I want to grow beans as food, not to collect and catalogue. I want to grow the beans that will provide us with a variety of different dishes, textures and flavours as well as cropping successfully in the UK.

Beanz Meanz

Native Americans are thought to have cooked their beans with fat and maple syrup – the origin of baked beans. Today the world's biggest baked bean factory is located in Wigan, England – except the beans aren't baked, but steamed inside the can together with the sauce. The first mass production of commercial canning began in the United States in 1895 by the Pennsylvania-based, H.J. Heinz Company. When their baked beans arrived in England, they were first sold in Fortnum and Mason as a luxury item and their sale soon expanded throughout the country at the turn of the century. The first baked beans sold in Ireland and Great Britain were prepared in the traditional US style. But over time the recipe was altered to a less sweet tomato sauce without maple syrup, molasses or brown sugar. The exact recipe remains secret and includes three spices that are delivered to the factory in separate plain bags to maintain the secrecy. The beans produced for the British market are substantially different to the nearest equivalent American Heinz product.

'Zolfino'

chapter 3

Beans for a healthy diet

Beans are good for us – without a doubt – and it is important to understand just how valuable beans are for a healthy diet.

If we are to ensure a secure, healthy food supply for a growing world population then diets must change dramatically to increase the consumption of foods such as fruit, vegetables, nuts and of course pulses. Here in Britain, and elsewhere in the world, poor diet leads to a range of health problems that create avoidable costs to our healthcare systems and is a leading cause of premature death. The necessary changes in diet mean there will have to be a considerable reduction in less healthy foods such as added sugars and red meat.

All beans are a good source of protein compared to other plant-based products and a helping of beans will substitute for the meat and dairy intake that we should be reducing. Only 25-40% of beans (depending on the variety) is protein, the rest is mostly carbohydrate. However, the carbohydrate content includes soluble and insoluble fibre and these starchy carbohydrates are much better for us than sugary carbohydrates. What's more the fibre promotes digestive health, speeding up the passage of food through our systems, helping to remove toxins and assisting with regularity. Beans are low in fat and what fat they do contain is made up of healthy monounsaturated and polyunsaturated fats.

If that's not enough, beans are packed with vitamins and minerals. Most types of bean contain iron, which makes them important for vegetarians who do not get an animal source of iron. They contain B vitamins and traces of minerals such as potassium, copper, magnesium and zinc. White beans are a useful non-dairy source of calcium. Black and purple beans contain antioxidants which help in the prevention of diseases such as cancer.

However, while beans may have that all-important protein content, they possess an incomplete set of amino acids. What all pulses are missing can mostly be found in rice and other cereals. This is why beans and grains, across cultures and continents, are often eaten together. Beans and rice, beans and pasta, beans on toast are staple foods in many cuisines – although it is now known that you can eat the complementary proteins in different meals with the same benefits. In addition, if combined with other grains, the body is better able to absorb iron and other minerals found in pulses. Another way of increasing the body's ability to absorb iron is to combine pulses with vitamin C rich foods; sprinkling lemon juice on a bean salad for example.

Some people, if they are not used to eating beans, can experience some digestive discomfort and it is the insoluble fibre that is the culprit here. The soaking and the way beans are prepared can help with digestion and so towards the end of the book I've added some practical information about preparation and cooking (see p. 117).

10 reasons to eat beans

1. Low in fat
2. Low in sodium
3. Good source of iron
4. High source of protein
5. Excellent source of fibre
6. Excellent source of folate
7. High source of potassium
8. Low glycemic index
9. Cholesterol-free
10. Gluten-free

In 2019 the EAT-Lancet Commission on Food, Planet, Health gathered more than 3,000 scientific papers that looked at the health benefits of eating one serving per day or more of beans, peas, chickpeas or lentils and carried out an analysis of all their findings. Here is a summary of these health benefits:

Obesity

Obesity is a growing problem and beans can be part of the solution. The fibre, protein and complex carbohydrates in beans not only leaves you feeling fuller, but you feel full for longer. This effect of feeling more satisfied and for longer helps in weight management, particularly by preventing snacking between meals.

Diabetes

Blood sugar levels rise at different speeds according to the foods that we have eaten. Beans are digested slowly and so the blood sugar levels rise and fall at a steady pace, instead of the sudden rise and falls that can result from other foods. Blood sugar levels are measured on the glycemic index and the low glycemic index of pulses help people with diabetes to maintain blood glucose and insulin levels. This can be particularly useful in either the prevention or management of type 2 diabetes.

Heart disease

Where heart disease is concerned, increasing your 'pulse rate' is a good thing. Eating a handful of beans (or other pulses) every day (about 130g), as part of your diet, can reduce 'bad' or LDL (low-density lipoprotein) cholesterol by 5% thereby lowering the risk of heart disease.

Digestive health

Pulses are high in dietary fibre and this helps to maintain a healthy digestive system and reduce the risk of colon and bowel cancer. (For some more information about the digestive process see p. 118.)

'Bosnian Pole'

Beans, beans, they're good for your heart.

The more you eat them, the more you fart.

The more you fart, the better you feel.

So eat your beans with every meal.

'Tresnjevac'

chapter 4

Beans for a healthy planet

Beans are healthy for our bodies. They are also healthy for the planet. It's a win-win.

The same EAT-Lancet Commission on Food, Planet, Health I mentioned earlier brought together 37 world-leading scientists from across the globe to answer the question 'can we feed a future population of 10 billion people a healthy diet without damaging the planet'? The answer is yes, but it will be impossible without transforming eating habits, improving food production and reducing food waste. Food – and what we grow to eat therefore – must be a defining issue of the 21st century.

Too much at steak

There is growing awareness that our diet and food choices have a significant impact on our carbon footprint. By some estimates, food production as a whole (farming, processing, transport etc.) is responsible for one quarter of the world's greenhouse gas (GHG) emissions, and meat, particularly beef, is the worst offender. Becoming carbon responsible means that we must take a long hard look at diets and how food is produced.

The plain fact is that we can't continue to consume as much meat as at present. If current trends continue, meat consumption is due to increase as the world's population expands. The global adoption of healthy diets that include no meat or, at the very least, much less meat, would help to safeguard our planet. The animals that are reared for food – cattle, sheep, pigs and chickens – are estimated to contribute about six billion tonnes of greenhouse gases (GHG – carbon dioxide, methane and nitrous oxide) into the atmosphere every year. This could represent up to 18% of global emissions, although estimates vary.

The figures can be baffling, so let's look at it another way. There are massive differences in the GHG emissions from different foods. Producing 1 kilogram of beef emits around 60 kilograms of GHG emissions. Producing 1 kilogram of beans emits just 1 kilogram of GHG. The difference speaks for itself.

There are more environmental positives for bean growing beyond the reduction of emissions. They are water efficient for a start. For each gram of protein, the average water footprint of pulses is much, much less than that of meat and less than many cereal and other vegetable crops. Producing dried beans requires less water than, for instance, those Kenyan-grown, water-guzzling slim green beans found on supermarket shelves. They require much less, if any, fertiliser in comparison with many food crops and when grown organically by gardeners and smallholders, that would be homemade compost only.

If properly stored, dried beans remain edible for several years, so they do not use up energy for refrigeration or freezing. Since dried beans are shelf-stable, the proportion of food waste at the consumption stage due to spoilage is very low, which also helps to ensure household food security. Additionally, many bean seeds are still able to germinate after

being stored for a long period, allowing gardeners, if they so wish, to keep beans for more than a single year and plant them in later seasons.

There are also important ethical issues that should drive changes in food production. Pulses already play an important role in food security in the developing world. By preventing the rich societies in the world from taking more of their fair share of the earth's resources, it benefits everyone worldwide.

In short, and I know I'm at risk of overstating the argument, in a world where climate change, biodiversity loss, food security, and diet-related illnesses are major concerns, changing diets may be one of the single most effective things we can do, as individuals, to build a better future.

The power is on our plates and in our veg plots.

Soil health

As if that's not enough, beans have one more great advantage: nitrogen fixing.

Even though the earth's atmosphere is almost 80% nitrogen, most living organisms are unable to use the nitrogen gas. Legumes work together with soil bacteria, rhizobia, to take atmospheric nitrogen found in soil air spaces and transform it into a plant-available form through a process of biological nitrogen fixation (BNF). Neither bacteria nor legumes can do this process alone, their relationship is symbiotic. Rhizobia cause root nodules to form thus providing the plant with the transformed nitrogen it needs in exchange for some carbohydrates made by the plant. The nodules absorb nitrogen from the soil air and convert it into a usable form that plants can take up for their own growth. In this way they are able to produce a high protein foodstuff by converting nitrogen in the atmosphere into the amino acids we require in our diet.

The nodules are most visible when the bean plant is just beginning to flower. So you'd need to dig up a flowering plant to check. If there are no nodules (lumpy growths of varying sizes and numbers, depend-ing on the variety of bean) then either there are not the right bacteria in the soil, or the soil has too much nitrogen already. Without nodules the beans are not fixing atmospheric nitrogen, but using what is in

The fibrous roots of a plant about to flower showing the nodules.

the soil. Therefore giving excess nitrogen-rich fertiliser or large quantities of compost will prevent the formation of nodules because the plants simply do not need to fix atmospheric nitrogen. So in most organic crop rotations, more nitrogen is likely to be fixed from the atmosphere when beans follow green leafy crops that have previously depleted the nitrogen levels in the soil. There are ways that rhizobium bacteria can be added, but good organic gardening, using natural composts and the no-dig method would seem to allow the bacteria to multiply in the soil. Other factors will also affect nitrogen fixation. The two opposites, drought or water-logged soil, will affect the process adversely, so avoiding both in cultivation is important.

When the plants have finished in the autumn, don't pull out the plants, but cut off the leaves and stems, add them to the compost heap and leave the roots in the ground to decompose. Although the majority of the nitrogen in the form of amino acids moves to the seeds, the rotting roots still contain a small share of nitrogen that the next crop in that patch of soil can use.

Interestingly the bonus for crop rotation and soil health may be less that bean plants leave nitrogen in the soil, particularly if the crop is left to mature as beans because almost all the nitrogen is removed in the harvested crop. The benefit is more that beans can be grown in nitrogen-low soil, following nitrogen-heavy, green leafy vegetables and do not need additional fertiliser. The low nitrogen conditions appear to stimulate more of the nitrogen-fixing activity, turning useless nitrogen into useful protein.

2015 Year of Soils and 2016 Year of Pulses

The United Nations (UN) General Assembly declared 2015 the International Year of Soils and 2016 the International Year of Pulses to increase awareness and understanding of the importance of soils and pulses, respectively, for sustainable food production, food security and for ecosystem functions. Biological nitrogen fixation might be considered one of the most important biological processes on the planet. Close links were maintained between these two celebratory events, taking account of the symbiosis between soil and pulses for working towards Sustainable Development Goals.

'Schneekäppchen'

Beano

'I want a bean feast' demands Veruca Salt *in* Willy Wonka and the Chocolate Factory *and the slang word beano, short for 'bean-feast' brings to mind, for many, the long running British children's comic,* The Beano.

A bean-feast was primarily an annual dinner given by employers to their workmen and then came to more generally refer to any very lively party. In the 19th and early 20th centuries, the bean-feast often took the form of a trip to some beauty spot where the meal was provided.

> *'A BEAN FEAST—A few days since, a Gentleman Tailor, celebrated for his liberality, gave a rich treat to his men, at his occasional country residence. It was called a Bean Feast; but, exclusive of the Beans, the table literally groaned with Bacon, Cabbage, Cucumbers, and, in short, every delicacy that he knew would suit the palates of his guests.'*
>
> Kentish Chronicle (Canterbury, Kent),
> Tuesday 30th July 1805

So although these celebratory dinners were named after the beans that were served, the food on offer could be much more varied.

But, just to complicate matters, the origins of 'bean-feast' may have another source. As part of a Twelfth Night tradition, particularly in the Low Countries of Europe, a pie or cake was made containing a single, dried bean. Whoever bit into the bean became the 'bean king' and was toasted for the rest of the night. Every time the bean king drinks everyone else must roar, 'the king drinks!' and join in. There are a series of four Dutch paintings by Jacob Jordaens that show the ribald scenes of Twelfth Night celebrations.

chapter 5

A short history

Today, Europe's most widely grown beans are the common bean – *Phaseolus vulgaris*. This is the genus that has provided the most edible types of beans and the most fantastic variety. The common bean is anything but, and botanists are still trying to work out its domestication routes. It is fairly certain that beans originated in two centres of domestication in South America. One is the area referred to as the Andean region, another is Mesoamerica (the area broadly stretching from Panama to Mexico). Archaeological evidence suggests that the common bean was cultivated in the earliest Mexican and Peruvian civilisations more than 5,000 years BC. So the bean is probably one of the earliest plants to be cultivated as food. If you are interested to read more, Ken Albala has written an entertaining and highly informative book that covers the history of every type of bean in many different parts of the world.

Wild beans are tiny and flat. Over thousands of years they were selected until the domesticated seed became much more substantial and developed other desirable characteristics such as pods that did not shatter to disperse the seeds far and wide, less permeability to water so that seeds remained dormant and could be stored, and greater tolerance when growing to differing light conditions.

The year 1492 was of great significance when the exchange of plants between the Old World and the so-called New World began. Christopher Columbus in his journal, recording his first explorations of the Caribbean islands, mentioned that the people have 'beans of kinds very different to ours'. Many of the explorers who followed him, visiting different regions of the Americas, saw beans being grown and eaten as a staple food and brought them back to Europe. From their landing places in Spain and Portugal, beans then spread, quite rapidly, eastwards throughout all of Europe. The new beans would have travelled along trade routes or with officials of courts and church, and were probably first grown in monastic gardens.

Before the arrival of the beans from the Americas in Britain, and the rest of Europe, it was the traditional fava bean, *Vicia faba*, or broad bean that was widely grown. The broad bean will tolerate some frost and prefers cool, rainy weather and so is well suited to the British climate. For most of the population, meat and dairy foods were largely unaffordable and so fava beans and peas were staple foods. By the 19th century in Britain the wealthier classes could eat meat on a regular basis but low-income families still could not afford regular meat consumption. Thus beans became associated with poverty and humble diets, an association that still lingers.

Across Europe fava beans were largely replaced by the newly arrived beans. The fava has two disadvantages: its leathery skin and an unpleasant anaemia called favism which is triggered by an allergic reaction in genetically susceptible people of Mediterranean descent. The new imported beans were safe to eat and took the place of favas. The British climate was less amenable to the new bean and so they did not become such an established crop.

The runner bean, *Phaseolus coccineus*, also originates from South America. It is thought runner beans were domesticated in the cool, humid mountainous regions of Mexico. Unlike the common bean, *vulgaris*, these plants are more tolerant of lower temperatures and higher rainfall, although not as tolerant of these climate conditions as fava beans. Runner beans take their English name from the fact that they climb vigorously. In France these beans are known as haricots d'Espagne, a throw-back to their arrival into Spanish ports. Rapidly spreading across Europe, runner beans are known to have been introduced into England in 1633 by John Tradescant, gardener to Charles I. In Britain the tradition of eating beans at the green stage has resulted in the popularity of runner beans and varieties that have been bred for abundant, long, succulent pods, rather than their dried beans. In Europe, particularly eastern Europe, they have been bred to produce shelling beans with pods that are short, blunt and thin-skinned. The one *Phaseolus coccineus* I recommend as a must-grow bean – the Greek 'Gigantes' – has been bred for its giant white beans and the

String beans

Until the end of the 19th century it was more usual to store and eat dried beans. Eating beans 'in the green' is a relatively recent phenomenon. The older varieties of beans have a strong fibrous thread along the seams of the pods, hence the name string beans, as they are sometimes called. Due to their stringy, fibrous pods, the young pods were not very edible, or at least only once the strings had been removed before cooking. Indeed, to eat them at the green stage was seen as a waste because it reduced the dry bean yield. The first stringless green bean was developed in the late 1800s by Calvin Keeney in New York. It took him many years to breed in this characteristic. From then on the focus was on the selection of stringless varieties. Breeding continued to develop bean pods that remain stringless even as they grow to a larger size. 'Burpee's Stringless Green Pod' bred by Keeney in 1898 was the most popular variety until 'Tendergreen' arrived in 1925.

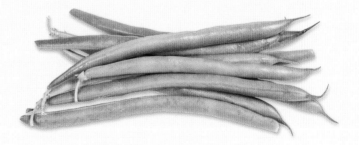

How the bean saved civilisation

Umberto Eco wrote in the New York Times Magazine *in 1999:*

'We believe that the inventions and the discoveries that have changed our lives depend on complex machines. But the fact is, we are still here – I mean we Europeans, but also those descendants of the Pilgrim Fathers and the Spanish conquistadors – because of beans. Without beans, the European population would not have doubled within a few centuries, today we would not number in the hundreds of millions and some of us, including even readers of this article, would not exist.

'Above all, it seems to me that this story of beans is of some significance for us today. In the first place, it tells us that ecological problems must be taken seriously. Secondly, we have all known for a long time that if the West ate unmilled brown rice, husks and all (delicious, by the way), we would consume less food, and better food.'

'Haricot Flajoly'

A line-up of pods showing the diversity of shapes and colours.

short, wide, leathery pod is definitely not edible. Interestingly there is a tradition of growing runner beans in some countries for their flowers alone – in Germany, Scandinavia and areas of the US, for example, locations where higher temperatures encourage flower production but discourage the flowers to set and form pods.

From the late 1800s as Europeans migrated to North America they took their beans with them, and so beans have criss-crossed the ocean at different times in history. Interestingly as European heritage seed savers look for lost varieties, they can sometimes be found in North American collections and repatriated.

There is one more type of bean that has its origins in the Americas, *Phaseolus lunatus*, which has a string of alternative names. Usually known in the Americas as the lima bean, in the UK this is what we call the butter bean. The name Lima is taken from the capital of Peru, a country in which they have been cultivated since around 2000 BC. By 1300 cultivation had spread north and by the 1500s its cultivation was widespread across the Americas although only in the warmer regions. These beans need warmer climates to thrive. My efforts to grow the beautiful, speckled, chestnut-tasting Christmas lima beans resulted in a total harvest of around eight edible beans from six plants. The plants sulked in our summer weather. They might succeed in a polytunnel, but when there are so many other wonderful beans to grow successfully, the effort to cultivate them just doesn't seem worth it.

The bean patch in high summer.

chapter 6

How to sow, grow and harvest

All beans seem to have been climbing beans originally, also called pole beans, and low growing plants would have been selected that have become the modern-day dwarf, also referred to as bush varieties. Some dwarf varieties, particularly heritage and landrace varieties, can still produce one longer leading shoot, a throwback to their climbing origins. Almost all commercially grown present-day varieties are bush because they can be mechanically harvested.

DWARF OR CLIMBING?

There are pros and cons to growing dwarf or climbing beans. If space is limited, climbing beans give a larger crop for the space they require. But they produce their beans later even if the overall crop is greater. Climbing beans also require supports, creating more work and perhaps expense if supports are purchased.

Dwarf beans reach the harvest stage more quickly but the bean pods are close to the ground and the plants may flop as the crop becomes heavier, increasing the risk of mould or munching by slugs and mice. For this reason they usually need some support; twiggy sticks is the usual method. A combination of dwarf and climbing varieties – just as I include in this book – ensures a continuous supply as well as the greatest range of different types of bean.

A few varieties of bean grow about 1-2m high (3-6ft) with branching vines and you can also pinch out climbing beans to produce the same shorter growth. At this height they can be self-supporting, but grow better if given some support up twiggy branches or simple bamboo teepees, similar to peas. Bear in mind that bean plants and pods can be heavier than peas so the supports need to be sturdy.

WHERE TO GROW

Beans need sun, and they will do best in the sunniest, warmest spots in your garden or allotment, preferably sheltered from wind. They do well close to a wall or building where they may get some extra reflected heat. They can, however, do well enough on 5-6 hours of full sun per day, particularly if the morning sun is strong and the shade is in the afternoon. Traditional varieties may be more tolerant of semi-shade, although perhaps less productive if grown in shadier spots or the beans will mature later. If your garden has areas that are part shaded, try the older bean varieties in those spots and you may be able to make greater use of your growing spaces.

It is a good idea to pre-warm the soil where the beans will grow by covering with cloches or plastic. Clear plastic (I save packaging) warms the soil faster in spring sun than black plastic, and keeps in that warmth well enough on cold nights. If your soil is clay and soggy, it certainly needs to dry out in order to warm up, so cloches work well. Leave the covers on until planting, as long as 4-6 weeks will allow the soil to warm up.

Beans will grow well in containers as long as they have enough depth. Some commercial containers are available, but very large buckets or big recycled tubs, storage boxes of any kind placed in a sunny position can be used. I use the bags that I grow the earliest potatoes in, and recycled compost bags stood on their end with the tops folded over do just as well (remember to punch holes in the bottom). The bigger the pot or trough the better as the soil is less likely to dry out and can provide a deep root run. As a rough guide a container that is about 60cm (24in) in diameter would support around four or five plants, depending on the variety. Some dwarf beans are particularly compact and suitable for containers. Climbing beans can also be grown in large containers but runner bean varieties are probably too vigorous. Grow bags could be used for the smallest bush beans, but they are too shallow for climbing beans and don't provide a

Dwarf beans growing in an old zinc tub. These are the flageolet, 'Chevrier Vert'. Any of the more compact dwarf beans grow well in large containers.

heavy base for the support canes. Canes are best to support climbing beans in containers, rather than sticks. Beans in containers do need very regular watering – check them daily. This is especially important when they are in flower and the beans are setting. Containers have the added advantage that you may be able to drag them into a greenhouse or polytunnel late in the season for the final growing and drying stage.

HOW TO SOW

In order to get a long growing season the seeds are best sown under cover, in a greenhouse, conservatory or on window sills in pots or root trainers. The pots should allow the beans a deep root run. I use 9cm square pots for almost all the beans, except the very largest and very smallest. Use a good quality, quite light, peat-free compost. The beans will grow generous, fibrous roots and the light soil encourages that root growth. Add some sand to the compost if necessary, to lighten it.

Fill the pot and then push the bean down with your finger to about twice as deep as they are long, usually about 2.5cm deep (1in), and a bit deeper for the largest beans. The spot where the root, the radicle, emerges is on the side, where the small depression, the scar, is and so the seeds should be planted with the scar pointing downwards. Although the root when it emerges will always self-correct to grow downwards there are slight benefits to sowing the seed in the correct position. The seed will use up precious energy if it needs to reorientate the root after it emerges and the shoot may emerge a day or so later.

Germination. The radicle emerges from just above the micropyle, a small pore in the seed coat which allows water to be absorbed.

Beans germinate at 15-25°C and should germinate in around 8-10 days. Below that temperature they will struggle to germinate. I often put the pots on a heated sand tray to give them a good start, but a propagator, warm window ledge or on a warm (but not too hot) boiler will also provide the heat that the seeds need to germinate. If warm enough and kept damp but not so wet and cold they rot, then beans germinate easily. If they seem sluggish to germinate, don't be tempted to water more, try raising the temperature. If you think mice can enter your greenhouse, make sure they cannot dig up the beans for an easy meal.

As they germinate, beans burst dramatically out of the soil and slowly uncoil. The common bean, *Phaseolus vulgaris*, pushes the bean itself out of the ground on a stalk and the seed leaves unfurl from within it (epigeal germination). *Phaseolus coccineus*, the runner bean, sends up a strong shoot and the bean stays firmly underground (hypogeal germination).

At this stage the bean seedlings are loved by slugs. Even if growing them in a greenhouse, be wary. When the shoots are visible, be sure

Phaseolus vulgaris. *The root pushes the bean seed out of the ground and it divides to release the seed leaves.*

Phaseolus coccineus. *The bean seed stays underground, the shoot emerges and the seed leaves unfurl.*

First growth in the greenhouse. Two bean seeds in each pot and the weaker plant is later removed.

Indoors to escape a late frost, under a grow light.

Seed leaves.

they are in good light or the plants quickly become leggy. Once germinated the young plants will tolerate cooler temperatures but will do best in a greenhouse or similar. Lightly water the soil and not the seedling plant.

Usually I put two beans into each root trainer or pot. Then if one bean doesn't germinate for any reason, there is at least one growing. If both germinate, take out the weaker of the two, being careful not to disturb the roots of the plant that will grow on. The easiest method is to firmly tug the unwanted seedling at soil level.

ALTERNATIVE GERMINATION METHODS

Bean seeds can be kept for quite a few years, up to five years, and still germinate successfully, particularly if they have been kept in cool dry conditions. But the older a dried bean, the less likely it is to sprout and grow. If your beans are old or you are not sure if they will germinate, it is a good idea to test a small number for germination before you plant them. Paper towels, filter papers from a coffee machine (which usefully form a double-sided pocket to hold the beans), cotton wool, vermiculite or any material that holds moisture, can provide a medium for germinating seeds. It is crucial to keep the bean seeds constantly damp but not over-wet, or they may grow mould. Place everything in a plastic bag to prevent drying out and keep the packs indoors where it's warm. If the seeds are viable, the seeds will first swell and then a tiny root will emerge – usually within a few days. If after about a week, you see no sign of any roots, then the chances are the beans will never sprout. If only about half or fewer of the beans have germinated, it is probably not worth sowing the beans, unless they are the only few left of a particular variety that you want to grow.

If sowing some favourite beans that you know have a low germination rate, it is a good idea to use the paper towel germination method and then only plant the ones that sprout. The only problem with this method is that you have to handle the sprouting beans very carefully in order to avoid damaging the delicate white root; it's very easy to knock off the tiny root. Make a finger hole and gently insert the bean. This is quite a fiddle if you have many beans to plant, but for that special bean, it can be worthwhile.

WHEN TO SOW

Bean plants are sensitive to frost and need warm soil to thrive, so sowing and planting out early isn't necessarily worth it. But at the same time we need to maximise the growing season in order to get the beans plumped up and harvested, ideally before the rains come in September and certainly before the cold weather of autumn kicks in. Judging the season from sowing to harvesting is the biggest challenge with growing beans for eating fresh and drying. I usually sow mid-April, or even later, to go out mid-May and keep my fingers crossed there's no late May frost. If you live further north, sow at the end of April to go out end of May. If you live somewhere south where the climate is very mild, you can probably sow early April to plant out early May. However, the plants will sulk and grow slowly if cold, so there is little advantage in sowing earlier. Take a look at average first and last frost date maps for your area as a rough guide.

If you can wait, sow later and plant out in June, the plants will thank you for it, but you run the risk of shortening the length of time for the beans to swell in the autumn. I write this knowing that it's the right advice but not always sticking to my own advice. However, I garden on a south-facing slope in the south of England with a stone walled house sheltering the vegetable patch, so I can probably get away with putting my beans out earlier than gardeners in other regions.

Later in the year, particularly if you live in southern regions, beans can be sown directly into the ground once it has warmed up. This is obviously easier and with the quicker maturing dwarf varieties this may still provide enough time for the beans to swell and ripen. I have too many field mice who would simply thank me and feast on the bean seeds if planted directly into the ground. If planting directly in the garden, then pop two beans in each hole and thin out the weakest later.

During the last 10 years, the growing season, according to records, has been getting longer; on average 29 days longer than the average growing season during the period 1961-1990. That's a big increase. This increase is largely due to the earlier onset of spring and warmer temperatures into late autumn. Now whilst this is a worrying indicator of climate change causing rising temperatures, a longer growing season is just what beans need. Adjusting to climate change, while we do not wish it were

The compact plants of Hungarian rice bean growing in a reused module tray.

happening, brings changes to what we can grow and how we garden.

One option to ensure a full growing season can be fitted in before the autumn closes in is to choose varieties that are quicker to mature. For the most part, dwarf beans are quicker to produce their crops than climbing beans. Equally, some beans are tougher in damper, chillier weather and so can stand for longer in the autumn. Interestingly, as I learnt more about bean growing across Europe, it became clear that many of the bean varieties that are grown in the more southerly countries of Europe are grown in mountain regions where the conditions are cooler and wetter. So I have found, quite contrary to what you might expect, that many do just fine in our climate. What they miss is the golden sunshine days of a southern European autumn to dry the beans. But more on that later.

HOW MANY TO SOW

Since climbing beans have a higher yield than dwarf beans, and if you intend to grow a few varieties, one teepee with between five to seven bean plants may produce all you need for two people. It also depends if you are growing a variety with the intention of eating the beans at each stage: as green beans, shelling beans and then dried beans. If this is your plan, you may need to sow more plants. Not all varieties are this flexible, remember, some are not good to eat as green beans and are only for growing on as shelling or dried beans.

The other consideration is the length of time before they produce a harvest. A whole crop of bush beans might only take around two months, whereas climbing beans will take longer. For dwarf beans, I usually grow short double rows of around 2m (6ft) long, with maybe 16 or more plants across both rows. (The spacing depends on the variety.) My preference is to grow many different varieties for different purposes. In this book I have suggested a mix of beans – some dwarf that can also crop first as green beans early in the season, and others that will be big, rampant climbing beans that produce only beans for shelling and drying late in the year. Equally, a crop of quick maturing dwarf beans can be slotted in mid-summer or even into the autumn if you have a polytunnel or large enough greenhouse. Aim for flexibility and different bean crops at different times of the year.

Planting out, released from the pot, showing the fibrous root system.

Climbing beans, ready to plant out at the base of sticks. A layer of compost had been spread onto the ground during the winter.

PLANTING OUT

The beans are usually transplanted when they have at least two adult leaves, although this is just a rough guide. If the weather is poor, I may leave the plants to grow a little larger before planting out, or if the weather is good, I may plant out when the adult leaves are just starting. Older plants will take more time to establish, so it's a careful judgement between size of plant and weather conditions. Always plant before the roots have used all the available compost, which is why it's important the pot size is large enough from the start. If you see leaves getting a yellow or purple tinge, meaning they have exhausted the compost, that is a sign they need to be planted out.

Before planting out, the beans need to be hardened off carefully for a week or more (again, depending on the weather) by putting the trays of plants outside during the day and back into the greenhouse at night. I usually move them in and out of the greenhouse for a few days, and then use a cold frame for the final few days. Depending on the weather

Borlotti beans, newly transplanted.

Climbing beans, starting to wind their way up the poles. Trailing squash plants and self-seeded rocket and red orach share the same patch.

and soil warmth, I may transplant out and then cover with a cloche while they get established. Once planted out, beans can, however, sulk for a while, and may need cosseting, particularly at night if the temperature drops or there's a cold wind. I have a tendency to put my bean plants out too early – I'm too impatient and never seem to learn – and then have to keep them covered under cloches and sometimes extra insulation of fleece or cardboard if it's cold at night.

I often read that beans don't like to be transplanted. In my experience they transplant without a problem as long as they've been grown in a large enough pot, if they are planted out before the roots are cramped and if you take care to keep the soil ball intact. Watering the soil in the pots well before planting out not only helps them get established, but also helps to hold the roots firm and undisturbed as you turn them out. Their fibrous root system is quite fragile. Growing beans in biodegradable coir pots or homemade newspaper pots means that the whole pot can be planted to avoid disturbing the plant roots. I offer this

Two rows of 'Zolfini' beans growing thick and fast, supported by twiggy sticks.

information but I have not done it in practice because in my experience if grown in reusable pots and carefully turned out there is little risk of root disturbance.

Dwarf beans are usually planted about 15-25cm (6-10in) apart with 35-40cm (14-18in) between the rows or you can plant them in blocks, 15-30cm (6-12in) apart in all directions. Spacing depends on the size of the plants. The diminutive rice bean can be planted quite close together, whereas the straggly Italian 'Zolfino' needs much more space. I usually plant any dwarf beans which produce a long single leader in rows with generous spacing so that I can provide enough support. Spacing the plants far enough apart for the air to circulate is also important, so that the plants remain healthy. You will need space at the harvesting stage as you hunt around the plants for ripe beans to pick. All in all, I tend to plant out with quite wide spacing because I'm growing them for plump, generous pods of beans and so the plants need to grow to full maturity and size.

The spacing of climbing beans depends in part on the type of support structure. The vigorous 'Gigantes' need a good 30cm (12in) between plants or even more. The slighter climbing beans that send up a single vine, can be planted much closer, even as close as 15cm (6in), although I tend to space wider than that. Again, given that I am growing beans to produce pods that will swell and dry, I prefer to give the plants space – for that all-important air circulation.

Most beans will twine around their supports in an anti-clockwise direction, so if you are helping the young long leader shoots to find their poles, bear this in mind. But runner beans like to be different, twisting clockwise as they wind their way up towards the sun.

SOIL NEEDS

Beans do not tolerate wet, heavy soil. The roots may rot and the plant will struggle to thrive. The fibrous bean roots need to get into the soil and spread outwards. If the soil is not free draining, one option is to create small mounds to plant the beans into as this helps drainage and offers the roots loose soil in which to expand.

However, they thrive with some compost, but do not need large quantities. The plants benefit from this moderate amount of compost before the root nodules have formed to support good early leaf growth. Too much nitrogen-rich compost will create leafy plants at the expense of flowering and pod formation. Compost also lightens up the soil while at the same time holding the moisture. I simply put a layer of my own well-rotted garden compost on the surface of the soil in the autumn, according to the no-dig method, and plant the beans into this layer.

When gardeners are trying to get maximum crops from basic green beans, then the digging of trenches and backfilling with lots of compost has been recommended practice, but with the no-dig method, this is not advised. With good soil, surface spread compost gives a good crop. Bear in mind, too, that some of the beans grown in European mountain conditions are cultivated in thin, quite poor soils and these soil conditions contribute to the flavour and texture.

Although I weed around the bean plants every now and then and my homemade compost often produces a blizzard of weed seedlings, I'm not too fussed to keep them completely clear of weeds. Climbing beans in particular soon climb free of any interference from the smaller annual weeds.

As they grow on, potash supports flower and pod formation. Sources of potash are comfrey leaves either made into a liquid feed with the most foul smell imaginable, or added to the compost heap. I add comfrey leaves and some wood ash to my compost heaps at regular intervals. Alternatively comfrey leaves can be added as a mulch around the base of plants and they rot down gradually releasing their nutrients – also helping to retain moisture that the swelling beans will need.

WATERING

Beans grow well when they have just the right moisture content in their soil; not waterlogged, but also not too dry. During dry weather water the beans well, and this is particularly important when the flowers are setting and the pods are starting to form. Water the soil around the plants thoroughly but not too frequently. A good soak every now and then encourages roots to grow deeper. Light, frequent waterings encourage surface roots that are then more susceptible to drying out. I use a simple hosepipe without any whizzy attachments so that I can deliver the full flow just where I want it on the soil and avoid wasting water or getting the leaves wet. Wet leaves and pods can lead to mildew and moulds.

COMMON PROBLEMS

Beans are relatively trouble free. One of the commonest problems is planting too early so that they get knocked back by the cold. This can result in weak growth and a dull, yellow look to the leaves.

Slugs and snails

They may feed on young plants, particularly if you are direct sowing into the soil. You'll see the tell-tale slime trail on the soil and on the leaves. These troublesome munchers may also be present in your greenhouse if you are not careful. Since bean plants are planted out singly, it is quite easy to surround them with a barrier of sawdust, eggshell or copper tape or anything else you know works. Young plants that are planted out are more robust and will survive the odd slug munching. But slugs may eat right through the stem, so it's still wise to protect them.

Greenfly or blackfly

They may colonise the soft shoot tips of plants or on leaves. They suck sap and excrete sticky honeydew, encouraging the growth of black sooty mould. Use your finger and thumb to squash aphid colonies or use a biological control. Sometimes you can wash off blackfly by squirting water at them from the hose pipe.

Fungal diseases

These may occasionally affect beans, such as halo blight. As its name implies, halo blight is easily identified by the yellow halo that forms around red-brown lesions, which are visible on both sides of the bean leaves. Other symptoms include the red-brown lesions alone, dark sunken lesions on pods and a cream-coloured bacterial ooze from the pod lesions. If the plants are infected, the bean seeds will be infected meaning that you cannot save the seed to resow.

This bacteria is most prolific when the weather is humid and temperatures lower. It's worth stressing again that good plant hygiene is important – trying not to splash water onto the plant leaves when watering and spacing plants apart so that any infected plants would be less likely to transmit the disease. If you have had one year with halo blight, be sure not to grow beans in that same patch for three years. Practise good crop rotation.

Treatment can be by removing and burning affected plants. Pick off all the affected leaves if plants are less affected or use a copper-based bactericide if you prefer. This can help beans from developing halo blight but it won't cure an infection.

Bean weevils

These are originally native to Central America, however imports of grain in the 19th century introduced the species to Europe and further afield. It's mainly a problem in warmer climates, and in England it is thankfully rare and confined mainly to southeast England. It's a serious pest of beans because the larvae of bean weevils infest the seeds, living inside until they pupate just below the surface and then emerge, leaving the tell-tale small holes. To be on the safe side, any bean seeds obtained from less reliable sources and grown originally in warmer climates can be frozen for up to a week to kill weevil eggs or larvae.

HARVESTING

If you have read through the earlier sections, then you will know by now that some beans can be eaten first as green pods, then fresh shelling beans and finally dried, stored and cooked to eat later. Some are only good eaten as fresh shelling beans or dried because the pods are papery and stringy. Even at the fresh, shelling stage there is a subtle difference between fresh beans and semi-dry beans, picked at the point when they are just starting to dry in the pod. The 'Coco de Paimpol' beans for example are traditionally harvested at the semi-dry stage to be cooked fresh. These variations of fresh, half-dry or dry open up a range of possibilities that are not well appreciated in our gardening and culinary traditions.

Pods gradually changing colour. These are 'Zolfini' beans.
The beans can be shelled and eaten fresh when the beans feel
plump inside pale green pods. They can be eaten fresh at the
demi-sec stage when the pods are turning yellow to light brown.
When brown the pods are picked and dried.

Fresh: Harvest when the beans are well developed and the pods are still green. They can be fiddly to shell. The beans will cook quickly, like fresh peas. They will keep in the fridge for a few days, or pop them in a bag in the freezer.

Half-dry – or demi-sec: Harvest when the pods have changed colour, or are just starting to change colour, but are not yet dry. The beans will be larger, a little firmer and will take a bit longer to cook than fresh beans. As with fresh beans, they will keep in the fridge. They are easy to freeze.

Dry: Harvest when the pods are dry – or starting to dry. Dry the pods, or shell and let the beans dry completely before storing. They have a long shelf life and will need soaking and then cooking for a longer time.

We like to eat fresh or half-dry shelled beans the most and will pick them to use in this way, putting any extra straight into the freezer in bags. There is a narrow window when the beans can be harvested as demi-sec shelling beans. Again, it depends on the variety and the growing conditions that year but generally around the early part of September keep a close eye on beans you want to eat fresh.

When harvesting it is best to use scissors or secateurs as the pod stalks can be tough to pick by hand. Tugging to pick the beans can result in breaking off more plant than you intended or even inadvertently pulling up the smaller plants.

Beans you are intending to harvest for drying need to be left as long as possible. If the weather is fine, and if the beans are developing well, then the pods start to thin and turn leathery, and with most varieties turn brown. The colouration depends on the type, and also the weather. As they turn brown, they will hopefully also start to dry. I rarely find this is possible in our British climate, particularly with the

Harvested 'Gigantes' pods. September had been dry and warm so these pods had dried on the vines. Some are still a little green and all need to be cured and dried thoroughly.

bigger beans. But if we are lucky with a dry, sunny late summer, some pods may dry. By this stage the leaves are yellowing and starting to drop. In damp, cooler weather it can be worth stripping off some of the larger leaves to allow more air to circulate around the plants.

Timing is key. Usually I check the plants every couple of days and pick the pods that are starting to dry. Not all the pods will ripen at the same time, so either pick as you go along and dry them little by little, or you have to judge the moment when most of the beans are ready. If the autumn is starting to close in, you might need to harvest the beans a bit before they are ready to avoid them becoming damp and possibly mouldy. That said, some varieties, particularly the climbers, can keep going right into the autumn if they have enough air circulating. It's the damp, not cold, that spoils them. I've had borlottis, Greek 'Gigantes' and Mexican black beans still standing by the end of November and providing beans that we can pick and cook straight from the plants.

DRYING

Even if the bean pods are starting to dry on the plants, the bean drying process still needs to continue. Drying beans can be achieved in several ways. The technique can be a bit different with dwarf beans than pole beans. With dwarf bush beans, if a lot of beans are ready around the same time, the whole plant can be taken up (cut at the root leaving the root in the ground), and the plants hung up somewhere dry and well ventilated. I usually hang them in the greenhouse on a metal cross beam. Alternatively I lay them outdoors on some old bulb trays; the metal mesh allows the air to circulate. If rain is forecast the trays can be quickly lifted into the dry.

With climbing bean plants, particularly the smaller ones, it might be possible to take up the whole of the plant if it's been grown on netting or canes. Beans that have been grown up twine or strings or fairly small sections of netting can be cut at the base or pulled out and then the whole bean plant strung up to dry on its string or net. With bamboo canes the bean plants can be cut at the bottom and then slid off the canes, bundled up and left to dry in a greenhouse, shed or conservatory. I prefer to pick the bean pods and dry them separately. Pods for drying

Dwarf bean plants, cut at soil level, hanging in the greenhouse to dry.

can be placed in wire or wicker baskets, or even spread out in shallow cardboard boxes.

The pods, either still on their plants or picked, are best left to dry naturally for a further few weeks; around three weeks is usually long enough, but keep an eye on them and turn every now and then. Ventilation is essential. Good air flow, rather than high temperature is the key. However, if the pods are sodden, they may need to be dried out somewhere warm, on the boiler (or even a very low oven) initially, before leaving them to cure more slowly. It takes a bit of experience and judgement to dry beans well for storage.

The beans do need to be completely dry to store properly. If you are not sure that the pods are bone dry, at the final stage put them through a dehydrator, in an airing cupboard or on a slightly warm radiator or boiler for a day or so.

Pods left to cure in a basket.

Overwintering tubers

Runner beans, Phaseolus coccineus, are perennial, but frost sensitive, so they die back in the winter. But you can save the tubers, overwinter them in a frost-free place and replant next year. If you grow a lot of beans, this may not be a practical option, but you could try it with a few plants. When you dig them up, look for the fatter tubers to store. Some recommend burying the roots in slightly moist sand, leafmould, or similar and packing into boxes or large flower pots. I simply dig them up with a chunk of soil and pack about six into a crate. I overwinter them under the bench in the greenhouse. Next spring I bring them into regrowth by potting up, watering and placing in the greenhouse. They can take a while to produce shoots, so don't give up on them. I find the plants get an early start and come into crop sooner. Try it.

Tubers of 'Gigantes' (Phaseolus coccineus) dug up and overwintered in the greenhouse (left) and a tuber potted up in the greenhouse and sprouting, mid-April (right).

SHELLING AND THRESHING

Once they are crisp dry, the pods can be shelled by hand. Since I do not grow large quantities of beans, shelling by hand doesn't take too long. It is a patient but rewarding job and doing it by hand allows for sorting the beans at the same time. Any that are discoloured or slightly mouldy can be removed and this method easily separates beans from chaff.

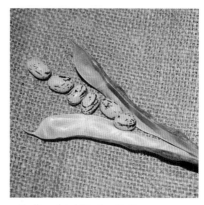

Shelling dried 'Mariazeller' beans.

For larger quantities there is a simple method using a cloth bag, sack or old pillowcase. Cut one bottom corner to make a small hole just big enough to allow beans out, but not too much chaff. Tightly tie this corner. Fill with bean pods and press and crunch with your hands. The aim is to open the seed pods, but not break up the dry pods too much. Finally shake the bag to send the beans into the bottom corner, open it up over a bowl and release the beans.

The next stage depends on the quantity of beans and how much chaff is mixed in. Picking over them and sieving might be enough to remove the chaff. Traditional winnowing methods involve placing the beans in a wide, shallow container, typically a winnowing basket, and tossing the beans for the wind to blow away the chaff. The modern-day alternative is to put beans into a large, quite deep bowl and use a vacuum cleaner set on a low blow setting or a hairdryer to blow the chaff over the edges. Use one hand to keep turning the beans as you hold the blower with the other. It's essential that the blower is very gentle, but this method works well, particularly with heavier beans. However, quite often it's enough to just turn the beans in the bowl and gently blow away the chaff, with your own breath. Don't spend ages picking over to remove every little piece of chaff. When the beans are soaked before cooking, any remaining bits of chaff float to the surface and are easily skimmed off.

Shelling dried black beans.

STORING

Store the dry beans in airtight containers; glass jars, plastic boxes or sealed tight in plastic bags. I store my beans in clip-top glass storage jars that have a rubber seal. Beans store best if kept in a dark, cool place with an even temperature. If they have been properly dried, they store very well until you want to use them but with time they will lose nutritive value and flavour and they take longer to soak and cook. Be sure to date them.

Conveniently, seed saving requires the same process as crop harvesting for dry beans, which means you only have to buy seed once (unless you accidentally eat them all). More about seed saving later in the book (see p. 134).

chapter 7

Supports
and structures

Climbing varieties – pole beans – certainly need some kind of cane, pole or netting structure for support. Fully grown bean plants, particularly some of the more vigorous varieties with big flapping leaves and generous pods, are weighty and so the supports need to be very sturdy. Many a year I have spent time creating structures that I am quite certain are going to be strong enough, only for a windy day to bring them toppling down.

The advantage of dwarf, or bush beans is that they don't necessarily need supporting, although it is a good idea to insert short twiggy branches to keep the plants upright. Whether dwarf beans need support can also depend on the variety. The small rice bean varieties, for example, are very compact plants that usually stand tall by themselves, or just lean on their neighbours. Some of the old varieties of dwarf bean send out half-runners, or a leading shoot that can sometimes be 60-80cm (2-2.5ft) long and needs a short cane, and some dwarf types are big sprawlers that certainly need propping up.

Also, as you search for pods to pick from dwarf plants, they can become loosened in the ground and fall if they have no support. One tip is to earth up the plants or bring in some extra compost as mulch and mound it around the stalk. This helps to keep the plants firm in the soil, improves stability and also stimulates some extra root growth.

Some of the climbing beans, particularly runners, are very vigorous. One trick I have read about is to shorten them by pinching out when they are young plants, reducing the final height of the plants and making them much easier to pick. I offer this old market gardening advice, but I don't do it. I'm sceptical that it causes the plants to put energy into growing several side shoots and delay flowering and setting pods. On the other hand, when beans start to reach for the sky, towards the end of the growing season, pinch out the leading shoots or cut back some of that extra growth, entangled at the top of the poles. Cutting the plants back at the end of the season encourages the plants to respond with more flowers and more rapid ripening of the existing pods before the weather turns. Also cut off any side shoots that are not actively bearing in order to encourage the set pods to ripen. Reducing extra growth, and even picking off excess leaves will have the added bonus of increasing that all-important air circulation.

In my rural garden, it looks in keeping to have homemade, particularly wooden and bamboo supports. Traditionally bean supports were constructed with coppiced poles, about 2.4m long (8ft) and around 5cm (2in) thick at the base. I have a sufficient supply of hazel withies growing in a small wood on our land that I can cut when the wood is green and pliable enough to form into arched supports. A hazel pole teepee is my favourite type of support and I think it's the easiest by far. Tied at the top with thick hessian rope, a teepee looks good, is easy to erect and is very sturdy. What's more, they are easy to move around. If the autumn weather closes in, the plants can be cut at the base and the whole thing, sticks and all moved under cover to dry. The hazel poles usually last two or three years before they become too brittle. Nowadays many people use bamboo, but spare a thought for where the bamboo has been sourced. It is likely to have been shipped in from halfway around the world. I am fortunate that a neighbour has a large stand of bamboo that she's happy for me to cut back for her every year.

'Alubias Negras de Tolosa'

METAL SUPPORTS

Metal supports can be a good investment if you intend to grow beans year after year, and particularly if you want the beans on their supports to look good in your vegetable garden (or even at the back of a flower border). Compact metal bean supports, the tall circular type, can be moved around more easily than more complex arched structures.

WOODEN POLES

Hazel – and several other types of tree, willow is good for example – can be coppiced to provide strong and flexible poles. A two-year-old withy is usually long enough and strong enough. The flexible withies can be bent and woven into arches or dome-like structures, particularly if you don't remove all the twiggy side branches, but use them to weave.

White flowered Phaseolus coccineus, *'Piękny Jaś' growing up a sturdy metal frame, with white sweet peas. Wild carrot (Daucus carota), grows in front, self-seeded from the wildflower meadow. Flowers and vegetables grow together in my garden.*

Preparing the bean teepees in March. The withies are cut before the hazel comes into leaf. I find that five tall poles widely spaced with a generous twiggy section above the rope, for five plants, avoids too much tangled plant growth at the top.

Thick hessian rope tied in a simple knot.

A bamboo teepee is a practical structure if locally-grown bamboo can be sourced.

Remember to cut poles around the middle to end of March when the withies will be pliable but not yet out in leaf. If you leave it until later in the year when you are ready to plant out the beans, the trees will have already broken into leaf. Cut the withies on an angle, and the pointed end will push into the ground much more easily.

BAMBOO CANES

Canes are perfectly straight and can be cut in relatively long lengths. They are resistant to weathering and can last for years. The thick, long canes that are best for climbing beans can be costly if you need a number of them. Bamboo canes also have the huge advantage that when the bean crop is finished, the old vines will slide easily off each individual cane. When you've spent an hour or more painstakingly picking bits of dried vines out of netting or twiggy arches, you'll thank me for that advice.

FENCING

I have a section of sheep proof fencing – widely spaced wire fencing – in one part of my garden, which I sometimes use for growing the shorter climbing varieties. You can use recycled wire fence along with sturdy poles to secure it, but most fencing is not tall enough for climbing beans.

CROP NETTING

Crop netting can be purchased for growing beans, but it must be strong enough to take the weight and again, secured well so that it doesn't fall when heavy with bean plants and their crops. Since I try to reduce the amount of plastic I use, I prefer not to use this type of support. As an alternative to plastic, jute twine nettings are available.

TRELLIS

A trellis makes an excellent bean support, particularly if recycled from some other purpose.

Short bamboo sticks in a criss-cross arrangement supporting some vigorous Dutch dwarf varieties, lifting the pods free of the soil.

'Schneekäppchen', one of the less tall climbing varieties, growing up repurposed portable sheep panels. Ox-eye daisies have escaped from the wildflower meadow behind.

RECYCLED AND RE-PURPOSED MATERIALS

With a bit of imagination, all kinds of recycled and repurposed materials can be turned into bean supports. The reinforcing mesh used in building work for example, makes a good support, and it quickly rusts to that attractive colour. Old metal bed frames or ladders can be propped against a fence or wall. I have some old galvanised sheep panels and two of these propped up lengthways make a very good bean frame.

STRUCTURES

Double row

This is the classic structure and consists of two rows of poles or canes about 45cm (18in) apart and tied at the top with string or twine. On windier sites the rows should be placed further apart at around 60cm (2ft) – or even wider – as this gives more stability. In each row, space the poles or canes at about 22cm (9in) or a little wider, particularly if your poles are for more vigorous bean varieties. Drive the poles well into the ground. This method is best with an extra pole along the top to give strength and stability. For added stability tie strings like tent guy ropes at each end to keep the whole structure more taut. It is often said that a frame should run in an east-west direction to equalise light on both sides, but I find it doesn't seem to make a noticeable difference.

Teepee

This is my favourite structure and is the easiest. As the name suggests the canes or poles are arranged in a teepee structure and tied at the top with a rope or wire. If the teepee is too large, then too much productive soil is left in the centre. Alternatively grow a quick crop of lettuce or radish in the centre space. The lettuce in particular will enjoy the moisture and the growing shade created by the young bean plants. Several small teepees, each built out of four or five uprights, can be placed in a row. Since I also like to grow several different varieties of beans, but not too many of each variety, the 'teepees-in-a-row' system suits my crop size. The only snag can be that one side of the row receives a bit less sun and light.

Maypole

For this structure a thick, tall central pole is driven into the ground. It needs to be deep and firm. Then ropes fixed into the top radiate out like a maypole and are pegged taut into the ground. My attempts at this structure have not been very successful, but commercial versions may work better than my efforts.

Arch

This is a very nice structure, particularly if it arches over a path. Commercial metal arches are the easiest and probably the most secure and although a costly outlay, obviously last many years. They can be heavy and unwieldy to move from place to place though, if you want

Taking inspiration from a woven arch and dome at RHS Wisley vegetable garden. The RHS team has a plentiful supply of birch, which is ideal for weaving into support structures.

Three sisters growing in Matt and Freyja's One Planet smallholding. The corn had a head start, sown a month before the bean plants. The beans are widely spaced among the corn.

to rotate crops. Pliable hazel or birch poles make an attractive arch, particularly if they are twiggy and can be woven into more of an arch form at the top. The weaving also helps to make the arch more stable.

Wall or fence

If you have a wall or fence already in place, then fix a solid, ready-made trellis or lean bamboo poles against the wall. If netting can be fixed to the wall or fence, it can be made to angle away from the wall. As long as the wall area receives sunlight for a good part of the daytime, 5-6 hours, then the beans should grow sufficiently well.

Three sisters

In the Americas, beans are traditionally cultivated with squash and corn, known colloquially as the three sisters – the three staple ingredients of the traditional diet. The beans' nitrogen-fixing capability provides nutrients to corn and squash plants, while squash leaves provide shade for plant roots to retain moisture and suppress the weeds. The corn stalks provide a strong upright stake for the beans to climb up, winding their stems around the main trunk of the sweet corn. The squash plants trail around the foot of the corn and beans on the soil. Since both squash and beans need plenty of moisture at the fruiting stage, and benefit from similar feeding, the watering regime benefits both plants.

More vigorous climbing bean plants will overwhelm the sweet corn plants and may even pull them over when heavy. When I have seen this combination growing in Guatemala, the beans looked to be the shorter, spindly, bean plants common in the drier, warmer regions of South America, with small, lightweight pods, and the corn plants were tall and tough. Selecting a climbing bean that is not too vigorous would be important if you want to try the genuine three sisters method. However I do grow two sisters together – trailing squash plants in between my climbing beans to make good use of the space and for the combined benefits to both crops.

The deer problem

In my garden deer are a problem, as they are for many gardeners in North America and in some rural areas of Britain. They have a particular liking for the leaves of climbing beans which are held at a convenient height for them, so I have to surround my bean patch with a high netting fence to deter them. Some suggest strong fishing line strung at one foot intervals between wooden fence posts. I have also discovered that growing squash and courgettes, trailing between my bean plants as the South Americans do, helps to deter the deer. They don't like to eat the big hairy leaves of the squash family and don't seem to step through them to discover the beans.

chapter 8

Six 'must grow' beans

There are hundreds upon hundreds of beautifully coloured, wonderfully flavoured beans to choose from. Golden browns, inky blacks, bright whites, purples and reds: beans that are speckled, spotted, blotched and striped and some that wink at you with a coloured eye. They are shaped like beads, bullets and miniature kidneys. There are tiny ones, little more than the size of a grain of rice, and giant ones, so big that just one is a mouthful.

In this book my focus is European beans. Many of them have been given special designations as gourmet beans grown in specific regions of Europe. Many of them have been gathered into collections of heritage beans, preserving the rare and endangered, with histories and colourful stories of their origins. But some of the beans I suggest to grow are fairly commonplace – the Greek 'Gigantes' for example are becoming well known and grown quite widely. So whether they are gourmet, heritage or very rare matters little to me.

For me the most important reason to grow a selection of beans is that they are good to eat and that they offer the widest range of culinary options. Each of these 'must grow' beans is a different type – one is large, white and creamy for example, another is small, dense and mushroomy. Another key reason I suggest this 'must grow' selection is because in my experience they can be grown successfully in the British climate. If I can grow them, with my casual gardening ways, then I am certain you can. The final reason I arrived at this selection is that they can be obtained fairly easily from seed suppliers, albeit with a little hunting. With current restrictions on international seed purchase, this practical reason had to guide my choice. There would have been no point in introducing the most wonderful Spanish black bean from Tolosa – which it is by the way – but then pointing out in the last sentence that the seed is almost impossible to get hold of. That said, following these 'must grow' beans, I go on to describe many more beans from different parts of Europe that require a bit more ingenuity to source but hopefully will encourage you to be more adventurous and discerning in what you grow and cook. Perhaps then demand will drive supply and it will become easier to obtain the seeds.

Nowadays there is an important shift in vegetable gardening. Among market and amateur gardeners, particularly given the need to increase food production during the war years combined with the tradition of showing vegetables, priority had been given to size, uniformity and quantity. Today's gardeners rarely prioritise these characteristics over others such as taste and texture and often prefer cropping over a longer period.

Every bean has a story. Every variety of bean is tied into people and places and is connected to local food cultures. I think that vegetable gardening books should tell these stories and be imbued with a love for the food promise every seed carries. Also, by knowing something of these 'beanlores' we create connections with what we grow and eat on our own soil. But I don't want to over-romanticise the heritage of beans, be elitist about beans with special gourmet status or create a cloud of nostalgia around rustic peasant life that was in reality one of gruelling poverty. Take for example the 'North Holland Brown'. It is a plain little oval, brown bean. It has no fancy gourmet status, it isn't rare or special in any way, yet is as hardy as they come and cooks superbly. Few people holiday on the breezy tip of Friesland in the Netherlands and come home with food memories that they hope to recreate and there hasn't been a Seeds of Holland company to introduce its delights. Interestingly I find this bean extolled in English vegetable gardening books of the 1940s through to 60s. Where did it go? Why did we stop growing it?

If today's seed catalogues include one shelling bean that is currently in fashion then they are most likely to list an Italian borlotto bean. There are dozens of varieties with wonderful names such as 'Lingua di Fuoco' (Fire tongue) and 'Centofiamme' (100 Flames). Among the many wonderful varieties of shelling bean grown in Italy, the borlotto bean is the best known and for good reason, it is both beautiful and delicious. So let me start on familiar territory.

Phaseolus vulgaris 'Borlotto Lamon'

BORLOTTO BEAN: 'FAGIOLO DI LAMON'

The best borlotto bean (plural borlotti) of all is said to be the 'Lamon' variety, so named because it is grown around a little village of the same name. The high Lamon plains near Belluno, a beautiful mountainous region in the Dolomites provide the right climate and fertile soil in which the Lamon beans thrive. In southern European countries, beans are almost always cultivated in the cooler, fertile and well-watered mountain regions and high valleys. They need these conditions, away from the heat and dry. It is the late summer sunshine to dry the pods that the bean plants love in more southerly parts of Europe. If we are lucky, we have glorious late summer sunshine, but it's not guaranteed. So in more northerly climes we have to pick and eat, or pick and dry.

The borlotto bean is a variety of the cranberry bean, native to South America, but bred in Italy over time to have a thinner skin. Speckled with crimson and pearl, they are medium-sized, chunky with a sweet, nutty flavour and a rich, dense, velvety texture. When cooked they sadly lose their beautiful colouring and become a light, fudgy brown colour. But in place of their colour they offer up a deliciously flavoursome, thick cooking broth. We often eat these beans fresh from the pod, cooked just with herbs, enough water to cover and a few glugs

Fagiolo di lamon

*The origins of the 'Fagiolo di Lamon della Vallata Bellunese'
(Protected Geographical Indication) – to give the bean its full
title – date back to the 16th century. It is said to have been
introduced in this area by Pietro Valeriano an Italian canon who,
in 1532, received some seeds as a gift from Pope Clement VII,
who got them from Emperor Charles, who got them from the
conquistador Cortéz, who must have got them from the Aztecs.
Whether the story is true or not we cannot know, but for a bean
to have its own legend says something about its significance to
the local people. Certainly as early as the mid-17th century there
is written evidence of its distribution in the Belluno area and
later, too, an Austrian land registry of 1862 records the bean that
was grown in Lamon.*

'Verdolino'

of olive oil. Borlotti beans are also wonderful for making Italian baked beans in a rich tomato sauce (fresh 'San Marzano' tomatoes are best – garlic and onion, perhaps some brown sugar and balsamic vinegar too if you like that flavour). Little can beat a winter meal of beans in tomato sauce, dark green cavolo nero and bread or sautéed potatoes. In the Lamonese gastronomic tradition, beans are part of numerous local recipes. *Pasta e fagioli*, beans and pasta dishes, feature in many variations. Beans with potatoes may not be an obvious combination but typical dishes, one called *pendolon*, mix the two. Borlotti beans also make an excellent purée called *menestrin*, which is good served on buttery toast or slices of garlicky bruschetta.

Freshly shelled borlotti beans.

Like many landrace beans, 'Lamon' beans are grown on small family farms. In order to verify that the production of the beans conforms to traditions and regulations, a consortium for the protection of the Lamon beans was founded in 1993. Traditionally the bean seeds are sown on 3rd May, the feast of the Holy Cross and the harvest should begin in the second half of August and end in late September. In my garden I can achieve about the same harvest time, usually starting to pick in the last week of August, as long as I have started the beans early enough. Of all the beans I grow, borlotti beans do need to be given a good, early start in a warm place to fit in a full growing season before the autumn sets in.

The 'Lamon' borlotti are climbers and grow quite vigorously around 2m (6ft) or more so they need good supports. There are some dwarf varieties of borlotto bean and they can be more reliable if we have a poor summer or if you live further north. The added bonus of dwarf varieties is that they can easily be covered by a cloche or fleece if the weather turns.

The colourful pods of borlotti beans, hanging freely under a hazel arch. In late season the leaves are yellowing.

If possible, grow the climbing varieties on supports that will allow the beans to hang freely and not get tucked in among the leaves. One year I used a metal sweet pea frame that then leaned dangerously to one side with the weight of the beans. But this had the advantage of allowing many of the pods to dangle clear of the plants and they stayed rot free and swelling in the autumn rain until October. Avoiding damp-causing moulds is the biggest late season challenge. I have also grown them on a hazel arch over a pathway so that the pods hang freely, allowing the air to circulate. Picking was a cinch and they looked beautiful, especially growing among pinky-red sweet peas, blending with the colour of the pods.

Borlotti beans are not the most prolific bean variety – although each pod is long and contains 4-8 beans – so you need quite a few plants to get a reasonable quantity. I usually grow about 10-12 plants, but then I grow so many different beans that I don't want large stocks of any one variety. If you plan on growing fewer varieties, then grow around 20 plants.

The large pods start green but as they ripen start to redden to the most glorious deep pink blotched colours that resemble the dried beans. The shells are not edible, so all the efforts of cultivation must be focused on getting the beans to plump up before the autumn sets in. Try to wait as long as possible, as rain will help them to swell, but if the weather becomes cold and damp, it can be a good idea to pick the pods, when still green, and cook the beans fresh. They will be tender and delicious, even if a little smaller. I rarely find they get to the stage where they dry on the vines. Usually I have to pick and pod the beans in stages, eating them fresh or drying them indoors. It is very useful to keep a couple of bags of freshly shelled borlotti beans in the freezer so that they can be cooked without soaking.

By mid-October, the rain has swelled the beans but the pods are wet and starting to brown. Time to pick all the remaining pods.

Phaseolus coccineus *'Gigantes'*

GREEK 'GIGANTES'

The name Gigantes comes, not surprisingly, from the Greek word for giants because these beans are huge, about twice the size of a normal runner bean. I'm sure these must be the beans that Jack swapped for the cow and that grew overnight into the beanstalk reaching high into the sky.

These sparkling white, elephant beans (as they are also called) are grown in the mountains of northern Greece and are much sought after by Greeks. They are the basic ingredient in the most delicious Greek dish of *gigantes plaki* stewed slowly in tomatoes and herbs. As with all landraces, production is in small family owned farms and the 'Gigantes' grown in Kastoria have protected status. In this area bean cultivation is a key part of the economy and its importance is reflected in local customs and traditions. The harvest is celebrated in a special bean festival.

'Gigantes' is a variety of *Phaseolus coccineus*, bred over time for these enormous pure white seeds, rather than for long, slender edible pods. It is we British who have preferred to breed runner beans to eat at the green stage whereas in eastern Europe they have been bred to produce large beans. The flowers are white, opening from pale cream buds.

I like to grow some white sweet peas among them on the same metal supports.

Coming from the mountainous regions in northern Greece and being a runner bean, they fare better in our climate than you might think for a bean grown typically in Greece. One chilly evening in mid-May my plants were 30cm (1ft) or so high, just beginning to twine up their supports. I merely propped some cardboard and cloches around their supports to give a little protection from the night-time chill. At the end of the season I can expect them to stand well into the autumn, even as the weather turns colder and wet. They are usually the last beans standing alongside the Mexican black bean – also from the mountains.

When sowing these big robust beans, they need a generous-sized pot to themselves. Sow two seeds into quite a deep pot – deeper than average if possible – and, depending on the weather and the right time for planting out, allow them to grow several leaves, even 30cm (1ft) or more tall. Recycled tall yogurt pots are the right size (with base

'Gigantes' flowers in bud.

holes punched) or square juice cartons with the tops cut off. The deep pots give the roots of these vigorous beans a good start and allow you to grow them on in a greenhouse or polytunnel if you need to wait until the weather is warmer. It may be possible to plant the seeds directly into the soil in the warmest parts of the country under plastic or fleece, but I've never tried this. Because these are not beans to eat at the pod stage, they must have a full growing season.

'Gigantes' in flower.

The plants grow fast and tall and need your most sturdy supports. They are likely to produce three or four vines from one root becoming very bushy. The plants don't produce a large number of pods, given how vigorous they are, but I imagine all their effort must be diverted to growing large beans rather than quantity of pods. Believe me, you will have enough beans, even if the setting pods look a little sparse. I give them a dose of high potash feed (comfrey is great) when they are flowering and starting to form pods in order to encourage a bigger crop. If the autumn starts to close in, as with all climbing beans, it can be worth picking off some of the leaves and 'cleaning' up the plants a bit in order to ensure air circulates and the beans don't get mildew.

The pods go yellow first and then quite soon after turn brown and papery. They are short, fat pods each containing only two to five beans. You can either pick and dry them pods and all, making them easier to shell, or shell from the pods and then dry. They are excellent to eat when fresh. When the pods are completely dried, they crack open very satisfyingly and the giant beans clatter into the bowl.

'Gigantes' in flower and the first pods setting.

Shelling dry 'Gigantes' beans. Cracking open the pods is an easy and satisfying task.

Phaseolus vulgaris '*Comtesse de Chambord*'
(*Hungarian rice bean*)

HUNGARIAN RICE BEAN
OR 'COMTESSE DE CHAMBORD'

How much more elegant the name 'Comtesse de Chambord' sounds than Hungarian rice bean. But the name rice bean gives you some idea of its size. This diminutive bean is an old original variety from, as its name indicates, the Chambord region in the centre of northern France. It was famously mentioned in Vilmorin's *The Vegetable Garden* from 1885. William Woys Weaver, a food historian, suggests that the French 'Comtesse de Chambord' bean is a slightly different strain to the original Hungarian rice bean. Whatever the specific variety, this bean is likely to be closely related to the 'Flageolet Vert', with which it shares a slender, oblong seed shape, very pale green colour and its high productivity. At the end of the 19th century certain vegetable varieties were developed specifically for hothouse forcing. The Hungarian rice bean was one of those. It is much too small for any form of commercial production, or even now for market gardeners, and so this historical variety has been maintained by private gardeners.

These dwarf beans are easy to grow, they don't need fussing over like some, and are prolific, coming to harvest in about 90 days or even less if early summer is warm. The plants, just like the beans, are small, dainty and delicate with bright green leaves. I find they can be sown in the large-size six module packs if you have some to reuse. If grown in packs they need to be planted out before the roots become too cramped. They will not grow much taller than 20-30cm (8-12inch), so they can be crowded together. The stalks can be a little fragile, so take care. I usually don't provide them with any support, but like all dwarf beans they can become top heavy with pods and might fall over. If they flop onto the ground the beans can spoil and in my garden they provide a tempting meal for field mice. I once found a stash of these tiny beans hidden under a large foxglove leaf.

Having been bred originally for forcing in hothouses, this bean will grow well in the greenhouse, particularly out of season and, being small and tidy, will also do well in containers. Equally the bean can be grown in cold frames, ready to cover if the weather turns bad.

Hungarian rice beans growing in a zinc tub. The sides of the tub provide support and the fine, pencil-thin pods hang over the side, safe from slugs and mice.

The Comtesse

So who was the Comtesse de Chambord who gave her name to these beans? She was the Archduchess Maria-Theresa de Modena (1817-1886), the wife and then widow of Le Comte de Chambord, at one time a pretender to the French throne. The connection with the Comtesse de Chambord is probably because rice beans were among the numerous forcing vegetables grown in hothouses on the large European estates.

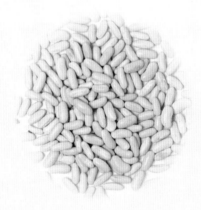

Curiously, I found some descriptions of this bean from North America that referred to it as a semi-climber to 1m (3ft) or so. When I searched more, I found a catalogue entry from 1901 published in the US listing it as a semi-climbing dwarf bean. My 1950 copy of *The Complete Gardener* by Shewell-Cooper similarly mentions 'Comtesse de Chambord' as a dwarf haricot bean of tall and rambling nature. These inconsistencies are very common in the naming of beans. The same bean may have many names or the same name may apply to what are clearly quite different varieties.

The plants produce many pods and these too are small, only about 10cm (4in) long. This is certainly a bean that can be eaten as green beans. If young pods are picked, the plants will go on producing generously. Each pod contains only eight or so beans, so when the pods have swelled, it is best to cut the plant at the root and dry the whole thing.

Once dry it can be very fiddly separating beans from dry pods. They don't crack open like larger pods, but have to be crushed and split. I pull the pods off the dry plants, put them into a large bowl and then crush them with my hands, a bit like kneading dough. Swilling the bowl will gradually collect the beans together, separated from the chaff.

Because of their small size the beans cook quickly, especially if fresh or recently dried, but even if they require soaking, they only need a short period. Mostly we eat them just gently cooked with a few herbs. They are sweet and excellent as a salad, with a little salt, lemon juice and olive oil or they can also be used like rice for stuffing peppers.

Rice bean and 'Gigantes', side by side

Phaseolus vulgaris '*Zolfino*'

FAGIOLI 'ZOLFINI'

In 1999 the Italian agricultural minister Paolo de Castro waved a small bag of beans in front of bureaucrats from the World Trade Organisation in Seattle. His purpose? To focus attention on a threatened and endangered legacy in the face of global free trade. The beans? The beans were the legendary 'Fagioli Zolfini' from the Valdarno area, a mountainous region in northeast Italy. The bean had survived in the plots of a few small farmers and was not sold commercially. It became a symbol of the struggle between the products of large-scale farming and large food corporations and the locally grown, regional varieties. In the late 1980s, production on a small-scale had resumed and it soon became known as a Tuscan agricultural and gastronomic speciality. The bean joined Slow Food Italy's 'Ark of Taste' in 2000 and is now grown more widely using only organic methods.

The 'Lamon' beans may be celebrated in the north, but it is the Tuscans who proudly refer to themselves as *mangiafagioli* or bean-eaters. Much of the traditional rustic cuisine of the region is based on beans. Cannellini, white kidney beans, are perhaps the most common and familiar bean. Other popular Tuscan white beans include 'Sorana', 'Toscanello', 'Corona' and of course the 'Zolfino'. While some cooks may substitute one white bean for any other, each bean offers its own individual shape, texture and flavour. Of course white beans are cultivated elsewhere in Italy and other parts of Europe, but Tuscany seems to be their home. It's interesting to explore the range of white beans and become more discerning about the differences.

The 'Zolfino' bean is not pure white. It has a sulphur-like yellow colour; zolfo means 'sulphur' in Italian. It is an irregular, roundish shape, and quite small. The distinctive characteristic of the 'Zolfino' bean is its very thin skin that prevents it from overcooking, and so it has a soft, yet dense, smooth consistency and good flavour. It is claimed that no other bean can stay as soft yet firm to the bite as the 'Zolfino' bean – although many growers make this claim for their own bean varieties. The very thin skin may also make it more digestible. It is

The cream-tinged flowers of 'Zolfino'.

'Zolfini' beans in early August.

also known as *fagiolo burrino*, buttery bean, or *fagiolo del cento* because it used to be sown on the 100th day of the year, around April 10th.

This dwarf bean is well worth growing if you can get hold of the seed beans in the first place. I buy bags of beans intended for cooking, and since these are recently harvested, I find they germinate very easily.

Alternatively the seeds might be purchased directly from Italian seed catalogues.

In their native region the 'Zolfini' beans are cultivated at an altitude of 250-300m (850-1,000ft), or even higher. It is said that they are happy in poor soils and do not do so well in lower, flatter areas of Italy where they do not tolerate the damper soil. They are sown on terraces below the olive trees, so that the water slips away. That said, the summer soil in my garden is often damp for long periods of time, and the beans seem to do just fine. I think it just shows how adaptable beans are to a range of growing conditions.

If landrace beans are grown outside their native area they are said to behave differently. In the late 90s, experiments by the Italian growers to produce these beans from more fertile ground resulted in a good harvest with larger sized beans, but with loss of its important qualities of flavour and texture. So our bean crops grown in our own gardens are likely to be a little different from the authentic Italian bean. What we grow to eat will always have the taste of our own soil, our own climate.

This variety is also said to be a bit temperamental, disliking extremes of temperature. It seems to be well enough suited to our English climate, at least in the south where I garden. The seedlings at germination stage are quite small and do need a bit of cosseting. Although it is a dwarf bean, the plants can grow quite bushy and straggly and will definitely need twiggy supports. Sowing to cropping, if the weather conditions are favourable, is 95-100 days. So as with all dwarf beans, the sowing to cropping period is easily fitted into our warmest months. The beans may be fairly small, but the plants crop well with a generous number of beans in each pod.

We usually cook these beans very gently in water until the broth is completely blended with the beans resulting in a wonderfully thick texture. Adding some herbs and garlic, and as always, a little olive oil – that's all that is needed. Serve on a slice of crusty bread for lunch or as a side dish. There is a tradition, *fagioli al fiasco*, where the beans are placed in an old fashioned Chianti-type wine flask – a *fiasco* – and cooked overnight in a wood-fired stone oven with the remaining embers and heat from the day's baking. Good luck with that if you give it a try.

Phaseolus vulgaris 'District Nurse'. The colourings of 'District Nurse' look similar to borlotti beans, but the beans are smaller, rounder and crop earlier.

'DISTRICT NURSE'

I think, if possible, we should aim to seek out and grow at least one variety that has some connection to where we live. In this way we not only help to preserve the biogenetic diversity and individuality of beans, we also continue a historical connection to the land close to us and its gardening and food production traditions. That said, the bean grown for shelling does not have a strong history in Britain – part of my motivation for writing this book of course and why I suggest we look to Europe for varieties and inspiration.

This climbing bean, named 'District Nurse', has a local history close to where I live on the Welsh border. It was grown in the mining valleys of South Wales more than 100 years ago. The story told is that Anita Bourne was given these beans by her step-daughter, a district nurse, who had originally been passed them by an elderly lady in Cardiff.

This bean has the prettiest lilac flowers which are followed by wonderfully coloured pods of green splashed with darkest navy blue. The beans are especially good when eaten as fresh shelling beans. They are light brown streaked and spotted with purple. The plants are sturdy, growing a single vine quickly to the top of their poles but not growing

'District Nurse': the pods are strikingly coloured.

over tall, soon diverting energy into flowers and pods. One year 'District Nurse' survived an unwelcome late May frost with just a simple protection of cardboard and some dried bracken. It's made of stern stuff coming from the Welsh valleys.

I find this bean is very productive. Although a climbing bean, and climbers are usually a little slower to produce beans, this one reaches the cropping stage in a surprisingly quick time. It is therefore well suited to our climate and probably a good variety to grow if you live further north. One year the beans were harvested, dried and the bean plants finished by late August. I would usually expect to be waiting at least another 2-4 weeks for the climbing bean crops to finish.

Phaseolus vulgaris *twine anti-clockwise.*

Phaseolus vulgaris *Black Turtle Beans.*
Turtle beans are typically smaller varieties of black bean.

BLACK BEANS

There should definitely be a black bean in any collection of 'must-grow' beans. A black bean opens up a range of dishes that call for the meaty, dusky, almost mushroomy flavour of these beans. The one I have grown for several years came originally from Mexico and so I am breaking with my commitment to European beans by including this one. There are, however, a few varieties of black bean in Europe, almost certainly relatives of Mexican black beans although they tend to be a little larger in size. The shiny, purply-black bean from Tolosa in northern Spain is one. It is simply that I have grown and kept the seed from beans I brought back from a bean seller in the backstreets of Oaxaca in Mexico, and find it does surprisingly well in my soil and climate.

According to the food historian William Woys Weaver, although black beans arrived in Europe from South America, their blackness as a food colour was not popular. Vilmorin in 1885 lists a Mexican black bean but states quite firmly that on account of its colour, it could only be used at the green bean stage and not as a dry bean. The inky colouring leached into other pale foods in a way that Europeans disliked. This could also be an explanation for the quantity of white beans across France and Italy, noticeably many more than in the Americas or other parts of the world. John Organ's 1960 book *Rare Vegetables* (of England) includes a Mexican black that he describes as an 'old dwarf variety that still finds favour' that he 'highly recommends for storing'. So this variety must have been around in England for some time and the black colouring acceptable to cooks.

Black beans – turtle bean is a nickname – have been grown in Latin America for thousands of years and are a staple food. This small, dense purple-black bean, *frijoles negros* in Spanish, is easy to grow and prolific. We cook them into refried beans to eat with Mexican dishes, or to eat at lunchtime with nachos. Black beans are also used in Indian cuisine. The dense flavour of these beans make them perfect as a meat substitute in vegetarian burgers or similar.

Black beans contain a certain antioxidant called anthocyanin which gives the beans their purply black colour and in larger quantities than any other bean. Antioxidants are compounds I mentioned earlier, which play a key role in protecting our bodies and may reduce the risk of certain diseases including heart disease and certain cancers.

The black bean variety I grow is vigorous and strong, growing over 2m (6ft) tall and with numerous branching shoots. One year they had completely covered their own sticks and partly taken over a nearby teepee becoming all entangled in its neighbour. As climbing beans they spend a lot of time growing vines and leaves and seem reluctant to flower. Each year I become concerned that they will be too late to set beans, and yet they do, producing their pretty, small lilac flowers well into September and still full of leaf, setting beans in October. One year I was still harvesting the beans in November. As with

Black beans have beautiful lilac-purple flowers.

many other beans I have success with, these beans are grown in the mountains – the mountains above Oaxaca in Mexico, and so they must be used to standing in chilly, misty weather. In the autumn, however, the bean pods rarely dry on the plant, so I either have to pick and dry, or more usually freeze to use fresh. Only at the final stage do the beans turn the deepest, inky black, before then they are every shade of pink through to purple. A dish of these lightly boiled, fresh beans has a wonderful range of colours.

Dwarf Black Turtle Beans, the short pods starting to swell.

A dwarf black bean variety is obtainable from seed sellers; it is a compact and better behaved plant than my rampant Mexican variety. I also suggest the wonderful black bean, a climbing variety, from Tolosa, Spain, that I include in the next chapter.

Shelled black beans in a range of colours from pale green through pinks and purples to black.

chapter 9

More beans from across Europe

There are many, many more wonderful beans to grow – and eat.

In this chapter I introduce more beans in the hope that I will encourage you to search for an even wider variety for your garden and kitchen. These are just some of the beans I have managed to obtain and cultivate and I am continually trying new ones. What I include here simply reflects my discoveries and is not intended to be a comprehensive list or systematic in any way. Some of the beans can be fussy growers, but the delicious beans they produce make the fussing worthwhile; others are easy, robust and reward with plentiful crops. However the challenge is to obtain the bean seeds in the first place, particularly for some of the more unusual European varieties. I give more information about possible sources of seed at the end of the book.

Here are the beans that I include in this section:

- Britain: 'Veitch's Climbing', 'Ice/Crystal Wax'
- The Netherlands: Friesland beans – 'North Holland Brown', 'Wieringer', 'Reade Krobbe'
- France: 'Coco de Paimpol', 'Tarbais', 'Chevrier Vert', 'Goût de Châtaigne d'Echenans'
- Italy: Beans from the Sarconi region
- Spain: 'Alubias Negras de Tolosa', 'Mongeta del Ganxet'
- Poland: 'Piękny Jaś'
- Austria and southern Germany: 'Mariazeller', 'Schneekäppchen'
- Slovenia, Croatia, Bosnia: 'Crešnjevec', 'Domaći Čučak', 'Bosnian Pole'.

Several of the beans I include in this section belong to the Ark of Taste. Recently, there has been international motivation to not only maintain crop genetic diversity but also to maintain the rich cultural and historical contexts in which these heritage and landrace crops are grown. The Ark of Taste travels the world collecting endangered small-scale quality food products that belong to the cultures, history and traditions of specific regions and countries.

BRITAIN

There are some, albeit not many, British heritage and landrace beans and I have already included the 'District Nurse'. I have grown 'Veitch's Climbing' and the 'Ice' bean, and am currently trying some more British varieties including 'Early Warwick', a dwarf bean known in England before 1890, which others report is reliable, hardy in our climate and crops quickly on compact plants.

'Veitch's Climbing'

Run by the family for over 200 years, at one time the Veitch nurseries dominated British horticulture. Today, the horticulturalist Caradoc Doy is an authority on Veitch and is trying to rediscover the many Veitch vegetable varieties. As he says, 'there was huge demand in market gardens [in the 19th century] for bigger, fatter, tastier, disease-resistant fruit and vegetables'. While we may be critical now of the demand for bigger and fatter if it sacrifices taste and texture, the Veitch family bred hundreds of vegetable varieties to serve the market garden trade. Only a handful remain, of which 'Veitch's Climbing' Bean, introduced in 1885, is one. It was, once, the most widely grown French bean in England but it is also good as a shelling bean.

I include this bean because it is a good variety to grow if you want an 'all-rounder' to harvest at each stage from green bean, to fresh shelling bean and then to dry. Like many of the older varieties, however, the green beans need to be picked young to be at their best. These plants can spend quite a long time producing leaves and extra vines before they think about flowering and producing pods. The beans are a rich maroon colour and kidney bean size and shape. Another reason to grow this variety is if you particularly like chilli bean type dishes but like me are less fond of the basic dark red kidney bean. They are also very good as rice and beans, Jamaican style, with coconut milk and ginger.

'Ice/Crystal Wax'

The 'Ice' bean is also known as 'Crystal White Wax'. The bean gets its name from the green pods that lighten with age to a silvery green colour that looks frosted. 'Ice' bean was originally bred by Dutch growers and then developed as a forcing bean for hothouses by the English. The Heritage Seed Library, who are maintaining the seed, date this bean back to at least 1882. William Woys Weaver quotes an Italian horticulturalist who reported several forms of this bean in southern Italy long before 1845. So this is definitely a bean with a long and complex history.

'Ice/Crystal Wax', with its distinctive white pods that tinge purple as they age, tumbling over the side of a container.

Because it was bred for forcing, the ice bean is a compact plant, like its rice bean cousin. The small seedlings produce three seed leaves, like a three cornered hat. The snag with compact plants is that the beans dangle close to the ground, so you may want to prop up the plants or grow them in a container so that the beans can loll over the edge. Being an old variety of bean it may produce short, straggly lead shoots that are best twizzled around a single bamboo stick, or allowed to tumble over the side of a tub. As with the rice bean, the pods can also be harvested when they are small or left to ripen to small grain-like, smooth ivory seeds. It is productive and quick to harvest, perhaps as quick as 50-70 days in a good season.

Knipselbonen

Some Dutch bean varieties are dried, pods and all. If we are aiming to store food in the most sustainable way, then the more foodstuffs we can dry for long-term keeping, the better. The beans are strung on lines for drying like garlands or placed on large netting frames. Then the dried bean pods are soaked overnight before being snipped into pieces for cooking – hence their name 'Knipselbonen', 'snippet beans'. They are said to have a unique taste, the rehydrated pods taste something like mushrooms. Snippet bean mash is a traditional dish made from boiled snippet beans along with spiced sausage and potatoes.

Even within the Netherlands (and some parts of Germany – updrogt Bohnen), 'Knipselbonen' is a niche food. These beans are eaten including the outershell, making them very special and rare.
© www.knipselbonen.nl

THE NETHERLANDS

A collection of richly coloured Dutch beans, including 'North Holland Brown', the two-coloured 'Wieringer' and small, speckled red 'Reade Krobbe'.

Friesland, a province in the north of the Netherlands is particularly known for a wonderful range of autumn coloured beans: gold, rusty red, liver brown, sap-yellow, pale lime and ochres. All are smaller beans growing on dwarf plants that are both hardy and quick growing, adapted for northern climes, toughing it out in wind and rain, and very suitable, therefore for our climate. While France in particular, and Italy too, has cultivated every shape and flavour of pale and plump beans, northern European countries have grown these richly coloured, smaller doughty beans.

'North Holland Brown'

Interestingly, my old English gardening books from the 1940s through to 1960s include the 'Dutch Brown', or 'North Holland Brown' as it is usually named. Eleanour Sinclair Rohde in *Uncommon Vegetables* of 1943 devotes two pages to this bean. She wrote that 'before the war few people in this country took the trouble to grow haricots for the sake of the ripe seeds, for unlimited quantities could be bought very cheaply'. She adds that the flavour of the 'Dutch Brown' is particularly good. War conditions brought the 'Dutch Brown' to prominence as a dried bean to grow for storing and it is mentioned in one of the

Dig for Victory leaflets. Clearly the seed must have been widely available to British gardeners at that time but catalogues no longer list it.

The 'North Holland Brown' is humble in name, humble in appearance. These small, oval, golden-brown beans have a delicate flavour and soften easily when cooked, creating their own thick, savoury broth – perfect for a thick soup, with vegetables and summer savoury added. Interestingly, summer savoury is called *bonenkruid* (bean herb) in Dutch and is supposed to help with digestion. In the Netherlands these beans are stewed and then crispy bacon, pickled onions and gherkins are sprinkled on top, with apple syrup sometimes added. They have a slightly sweet flavour, and their size and colour make them a good addition as a side dish to winter meals.

Phaseolus vulgaris
'North Holland Brown'.

I had been hunting for the Swedish brown bean, or *bruna bönor* grown on the island of Oland, Sweden and traced back to about 1650. But in spite of my best efforts at sourcing this bean I haven't been successful. I can see the 'Oland Brown' in US heirloom bean seed catalogues, but import restrictions prevent me from buying it. However, I am sure the 'North Holland Brown' is very like its Swedish cousin, growing similarly in a northern latitude in light sandy, coastal soils and crouching low to escape chilly onshore winds. The sandy soil warms more quickly than other soils in the spring and doesn't become waterlogged; something all beans hate. Everything about the 'North Holland Brown' is robust and unfussy. The plants, with leaves that have a faint gold tinge matching the beans to come, grow 30-50cm (12-20in) tall and produce many pods, about 9cm (3.5in) long with around four to five beans in each.

The US sites listing this bean suggest it makes a good bean for baked beans, preferable to the usual, bland navy bean. The Swedish use their *bruna bönor* to make a baked bean dish with vinegar, brown sugar

'North Holland Brown' crops well on stocky plants.

Mid-August and a first picking of 'North Holland Brown' for drying. The weather has been damp and I noticed the first signs of brown spots on some of the thinning, pale pods, so I harvested them.

and spices, which seems very like American baked bean recipes. I doubt there is any historical link between these recipes, but similar piquant flavourings for these beans have emerged in the cuisine of two different countries.

'Reade Krobben'

This landrace is still cultivated in a few areas of Friesland. *Krobbe* is the Friesian word for something that is very small. It is darkest, maroon red with speckles of yellow ochre and so I like this bean for its wonderful colour. This is a good variety to eat as a young green bean as well as leaving it to plump up to the shelling stage. The shelled bean retains its shape when boiled, less starchy and less prone to blending into a broth than the 'North Holland Brown'. It has a slightly spicy taste. The pods are surprisingly short, only about 8-10cm (3-4in) long.

'Wieringer' bean

It is said that the 'Wieringer' bean was brought to the Netherlands by the West India Company, probably from Mexico. At that time, in the 17th century, Wieringen was still an island that ships sailed past when they were en route to the Dutch ports. The story goes that one ship was too low in the water to sail through the channel and had to unload the beans in Wieringen. This is how the beans acquired their name.

For many years this bean was only grown around Wieringen. Being grown close to sea ports, the beans were often taken on board to provide food for long sea voyages, but then the variety was lost in the Netherlands. Ruurd Walrecht, a Dutch horticulturist who has made a lifetime's work of preserving heritage vegetable seed varieties, found the bean among Dutch emigrants in the US under the name of Wirringer. He introduced it back into cultivation in the Netherlands. The bean seeds were distributed to growers to propagate and multiply. These beans are white with a distinctive, yellow-brown patch.

ITALY

Of all European countries, Italy must have the greatest variety of regional *fagioli*. There are so many across the whole of Italy that it took two volumes for Gian Spaliviero to describe all the local varieties and their accompanying recipes. The north Italian 'Borlotto Lamon' and the 'Zolfino' remain my favourites, and so Italian beans have already taken up lengthy sections of this book, but there are many, many others to try. I have been able to source seeds from a range that grow in the Sarconi region, so it is these that I describe here – but they represent just one locality out of so many. I hope this motivates you to start your own searches.

Beans from Sarconi: 'Tuvagliedda Marrone' and 'Verdolino'

Sarconi is a small town in the Agri Valley, southern Italy, that is famous for its excellent beans. There are records of beans having been grown in this region for hundreds of years. Over time the local growers exchanged seeds, perhaps fascinated by their colours and patterns. So because they have been confined to one region for so long, the growers have preserved the distinct biodiversity of this one group of various beans known as the 'Fagioli di Sarconi'. Like many regions

Left: Phaseolus vulgaris *'Tuvagliedda Marrone'*.
Right: Phaseolus vulgaris *'Fagiolo Verdolino di Sarconi'. The name translates as 'greenish bean from Sarconi', although the colour is more yellow-green when I grow them.*

that have become famous for growing beans, the soil is a light, sandy loam, deep and fertile, with a climate that does not get too hot in the summer and offers plenty of water for irrigation.

A number of different beans are distinctive to this region; the 'Tuvagliedda Marrone' and 'Verdolino' are just two out of many. The 'Tuvagliedda Marrone' is a climbing bean with a round-oval seed, partly white and partly mottled with brown in a very attractive, uneven pattern. It's not the most robust bean in the British climate, but grows well enough to be worth growing.

The 'Verdolino', a dwarf bean, has a delicate taste matched by a delicate pale yellow-green colour, with an almost sweet flavour. The flowers are pale pink – an unusual colour for beans – the pods are short, broad and green and the beans quite small, plump and oval. Traditionally both the fresh, green pods and the shelling beans can be eaten but I leave the beans to mature. The beans are perfect cooked and mixed with small shaped pasta or rice because they are quite small. Although I usually reject the suggestion that beans, with lack of culinary imagination, can be thrown into soups or stews, beans make an excellent soup if they are the main ingredient. The 'Verdolino' beans are not too heavy and starchy and so they make a good soup, perhaps with some of the cooked beans mashed to make the broth even richer, and adding the usual glugs of olive oil and generous quantities of herbs and garlic.

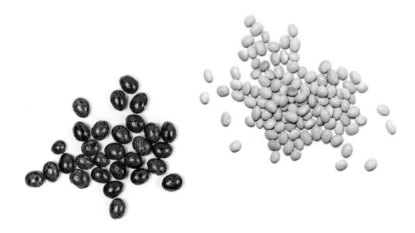

FRANCE

Like Italy, France is home to many varieties of bean, with regional dishes that bring out their best qualities. They can be usefully grouped into three types:

- Coco: medium-sized, round beans that are usually eaten fresh or demi-sec. Varieties include the famous 'Coco de Paimpol', also the widely available 'Coco Nain Blanc Précoce'.
- Lingot: large, white and starchy that usually need long, slow cooking. Varieties include the 'Haricot Tarbais', 'Lingot du Nord', 'Mogette de Vendée' and several of the beans from the Soissons region.
- Flageolet: slim, green, harvested a little before maturity. Varieties include the old variety 'Chevrier Vert', and more recent varieties such as 'Vernor', 'Elsa' and 'Flajoly'.

Here I include one of each type plus the rather unusual 'Goût Châtaigne d'Echenans'.

'Coco de Paimpol'

This bean first came to my attention because a top-notch English restaurant with its own kitchen garden had secured some to grow and serve to guests. Prized by chefs, this delicious bean is typically served with pieces of chunky white fish.

The 'Coco de Paimpol' beans are only grown in one small coastal area of northern France, the Côtes d'Armor in Brittany, where they have been grown since the 18th century. It is said that the climate in this area of northern France creates a long, slow-growing period that produces the thin, tender seed coat. In Brittany the climate is very similar to Britain (in southern counties at least) so this bean grows well for me.

Phaseolus vulgaris 'Coco de Paimpol'

The plants are dwarf but quite bushy and large. When they germinate, the seed leaves seem too small and a little crinkled, but the plants soon grow strongly. The beans are roundish in shape, white, but with a touch of cream, smaller than a borlotto bean, but larger and fatter than many haricot beans. The pods are quite large, a pale yellow/cream colour with attractive light purple markings.

This is said to be the bean traditionally used in French cassoulet, although several beans lay claim to being the genuine cassoulet bean. Any bean for cassoulet needs to be white, medium-sized and quite starchy so that it does not disintegrate completely during the hours of slow cooking the cassoulet requires, but retains just enough texture and bite.

In Brittany an army of pluckers, as they are called, harvest 'Coco de Paimpol' beans by hand at the semi-dried, shelling bean stage; for this is when they are at their best. This is definitely not a bean that can be eaten at the green bean stage, the pods are stringy and tough. Because they are usually picked and shelled when they are mature and just starting to dry (the demi-sec stage) the beans cook very rapidly, needing only about 30-45 minutes. Once picked they will keep fresh in their pods in the fridge for about a week or they can be podded for freezing.

A harvest of 'Coco de Paimpol' picked at the demi-sec stage.

'Tarbais'

This is the famous white 'Tarbais' bean, named after the town of Tarbes in the southwest of France. It is a creamy white, medium-sized climbing bean with a lower starch content than many beans, which is said to make them quicker to soften in cooking. They do not have the shiny skin of some beans, more of a matt, slightly wrinkled appearance. Notice how a majority of French beans are white and largish; a long-standing preference for pale beans and a rejection of black or very dark varieties.

Phaseolus vulgaris *'Tarbais'*.

Bags of dried 'Tarbais' beans for cooking are available from a few gourmet food sellers and are unbelievably expensive. They are pricey because the plants are not overly prolific and their cultivation is labour intensive. The beans dry on the vines and then must be picked by hand. The 'Tarbais' bean was, incidentally, the first bean in France to be granted the special status of 'Label Rouge' in 1997.

The long, generous pods of 'Tarbais' beans.

'Tarbais' seed beans are available from certain seed sellers, but they carefully stress that because it has not been grown in the protected geographical area, it cannot be considered the true 'Tarbais' bean, nor carry that name. As I have mentioned elsewhere, the specific flavour and texture of beans is also due to the soil and climate of a particular region, so if we grow a bean in our own gardens, it may not be quite the genuine thing.

Cassoulet

Cassoulet is perhaps the best known, classic bean dish in European cuisine. The slow cooked cassoulet originated in the southwest region of France and typically contains beans with pork, sausages, goose or duck. If the meat ingredients sound a bit excessive, particularly in a book that is recommending a protein transition from meat to pulses, it's important to recognise that beans are the primary ingredient. Besides, there are many non-meat cassoulet recipes which slow cook the beans with herbs, carrots, leeks, onions and sometimes other vegetables such as kale and artichokes. For me a generous sprinkling of breadcrumbs to form that wonderful crust is a must.

Bear in mind that if you do want to create the authentic regional flavour, a cassoulet should be cooked in a wood-fired baker's oven and the beans must be soaked in water from the spring which has supplied the town of Tarbes since the 1800s!

Legend has it that cassoulet originated during the Hundred Years' War. During the siege of Castelnaudary by the English, the townsfolk pooled everything they could find to feed the town's soldiers. Fava beans, bacon fat, scraps of pork and sausage were all stewed together in a large pan. Revived by this meal, the soldiers drove the English out of the region. So the Cassoulet was originally a stew of meat and fava beans and essentially a dish for the poor, using leftovers. The stew was cooked in a special dish called a cassole hence its name. The cassole is a brick red earthenware dish that is quite shallow and wide brimmed, allowing more beans to be exposed to the heat so that the characteristic crust forms.

'Tarbais'

'Chevrier Vert'

The 'Flageolet Vert' – or 'Chevrier Vert' as the heritage variety is known – has that wonderful pale pistachio colour due to its ability to retain chlorophyll longer than other beans, even when dried. As they dry, they become paler, so this is another bean that is best eaten at the fresh, shelling stage (*haricots à écosser*) or demi-sec stage when the beans have their freshest green colour. You may need to watch closely to pick them when they are at their best. This variety was first cultivated by Gabriel Chevrier (hence its name) in a suburb of Paris in the 1870s. A close relative of the Hungarian rice bean, this is another compact plant that becomes top-heavy with pods – just what we want – but as a result is particularly prone to flopping. Being compact, it can be grown in containers and the pods then dangle freely over the sides. Some of the more recent flageolet cultivars are taller and better behaved and probably a good option to grow.

Cooking needs to be simple, to preserve their delicate flavour and colour. This small, elongated bean is excellent in salads – almost the best salad bean I would say – or served simply as a vegetable side dish with tarragon and maybe a dash of cream.

'Chevrier Vert', a flageolet bean, freshly shelled.

'Goût Châtaigne d'Echenans'

Translated, the name of this bean means 'taste of chestnut from Echenans'. Echenans is in eastern France close to the Swiss border. I tried to grow Christmas lima beans for their chestnutty flavour, but without success; lima beans really do need a warmer climate. However in place of the lima bean I have discovered this heritage French variety that has a distinctive chestnut flavour. It is a tall, vigorous climbing bean that crops early and is very productive. It bears irregularly rounded, medium-sized beans in the rich darker, unusual colours of green, brown and purplish; quite different to the white, dense-textured cassoulet beans of southwestern France.

Phaseolus vulgaris *'Goût Châtaigne d'Echenans'. As the seed dries it turns brown. These beans have an unusual, irregular shape.*

Freshly shelled.

The flowers of 'Goût Châtaigne d'Echenans'.

SPAIN

Spain is home to many varieties of beans, all cultivated in specific regions by labour-intensive, traditional farming methods and inextricably linked to each of the regions where they are grown.

'Alubias Negras de Tolosa'

In the Basque region of northern Spain around the town of Tolosa, two quite distinctive, dark beans are grown. Called simply *Alubias Negras de Tolosa*, which translates as beans from Tolosa, one is dark red, almost maroon and the other shiny black with a tiny dot of a white eye. Both are medium-sized and egg-shaped. The dark red variety is a pinto bean, literally 'painted bean', so named because of their mottled skins; yellow

Phaseolus vulgaris
'Alubias Negras de Tolosa'

ochre mottling the dark red. These climbing beans grow to 2m (8ft) or more and produce abundant quantities of 10-15cm (4-6in) pods that typically hold six or seven beans. I only grow the black Tolosa bean because there are not many varieties that offer a larger black bean. I find, however, that it can be sluggish to germinate and takes a while before it comes into flower. I think it probably prefers warmth.

These beans have been part of local Basque culture for decades. Travellers from neighbouring regions had to pass through Tolosa on their way to France and so the reputation of these high quality beans spread far and wide. Until the second half of the last century, beans were a daily part of the Spanish diet. A rise in living standards and changes in lifestyle resulted in a reduction of the quantity of beans in the typical Spanish diet. Today, however, the diet is changing again as there is renewed interest in traditional Spanish regional cuisines. During the annual mid-November Tolosa bean fest, a group called the Brotherhood of the Bean produces huge vats of beans and distributes them as part of a four day event that includes cooking competitions, street performances and concerts.

The Tolosa beans make a warming dish in the autumn and winter months when the cold, misty air rolls in from the Atlantic across this part of northern Spain. That was how I first discovered the black 'Alubias Negras de Tolosa' on a visit to Bilbao one winter. In a small, backstreet restaurant I was offered a dish of just these beans, cooked with a bay leaf and a little onion, served in an earthenware dish. Two long, thin, pickled green peppers were placed on top. The beans were inky black in a velvety purple broth and had a dark, earthy flavour. These black beans could be substituted for Mexican turtle beans in all those wonderful Mexican dishes, although they are larger and a little starchier.

'Mongeta del Ganxet'

In complete contrast to the midnight black of the Tolosa bean, the 'Mongeta del Ganxet' beans are laundry white. They can be found in Barcelona food markets served in typical Catalan dishes with cod or with mussels. Considered the finest white bean in the world by many chefs and food gourmets, they are almost impossible to find outside of Spain. Luckily I found one seed company who had sourced it from a seed preservation bank in Spain.

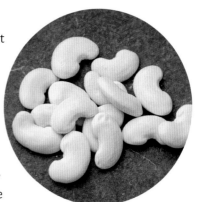

Phaseolus vulgaris
'Mongeta del Ganxet'

This is a medium-sized bean that has a very distinctive shape; it looks more like a cashew nut than a bean. It has a low starch content, making it quick to cook and light in texture and flavour. They are ideal for dishes where you want to highlight the flavours of other, quite light ingredients such as fish or vegetables.

The 'Mongeta del Ganxet' are cultivated in just one locality of Catalonia in the districts of El Maresme and Vallès. These tall, vigorous climbing beans (they grow strongly in my garden too, even though I'm far from southern Spain) are grown up bamboo frames in small fields and are left to ripen, crisp and dry in the late summer Catalonian sun. The whole of the dried bean plant is then harvested and threshed. They are also good if picked to eat at the shelling stage.

A Catalan bean

I asked my Catalonian friend Jessica about these beans and she messaged, 'That's a very Catalan bean, it's the most appreciated variety. It makes one of the most famous Catalan dishes, served with a huge sausage called botifarra. I can't find why they are called Mongeta – which means nuns – the strongest reason I can find seems to be because of the white colour of the dried bean. Ganxet means a small sickle because of the shape of these beans. That's very exciting that you have a treasure of the Catalan cuisine in your garden. Don't tell anyone!'

'Piękny Jaś'

Some beans have quirky and memorable names. *Piękny Jaś* translates as Handsome Johnny. Who was this handsome Johnny? This bean looks like a slightly smaller version of 'Gigantes' and could be grown instead to use in similar dishes. Like the 'Gigantes' this is a runner bean, *Phaseolus coccineus*, and grows vigorously tall and untidy. It produces the biggest, deep green, smooth seed leaves, like small, floppy cabbage leaves. Farmers continue to grow this bean

Phaseolus coccineus *'Piękny Jaś'. This bean is very similar to 'Gigantes', but a little smaller.*

(there are slightly different regional varieties) in southern Poland, in small fields, using traditional methods, mostly by hand. It's fascinating to watch short films on YouTube showing the work that goes into cultivation, particularly erecting the structures of chestnut poles and

elaborate frameworks of strings to support the bean plants. Bean pods that have dried on the plants are picked by hand as the summer wanes and then the drying vines with remaining pods are harvested and left to cure somewhere dry and airy.

Clusters of 'Piękny Jaś' pods on a rainy day, short and fat with only four beans at most in each pod.

Bee visiting 'Piękny Jaś' flowers.

'Mariazeller'

If you start to fall in love with the sheer beauty of beans with their myriad colours and patterns, then this is a bean for you. It is a quite large, longish typical bean shape, white and ruby red with a wonderful speckled pattern. There are possibly two varieties under the same name – one climbing and one dwarf: I have the dwarf. Many of the beans grown in mountain regions of Austria are hardy to colder conditions and this old variety from the Styria region, southeast Austria is particularly sturdy. I find it crops early.

Phaseolus vulgaris 'Mariazeller'.

'Mariazeller' are chunky plants for a dwarf variety, with oversized floppy leaves and large heavy pods, so they benefit from individual staking.

Phaseolus vulgaris 'Schneekäppchen'. Each one is a tiny snow-capped mountain that brings to mind the Alps stretching across middle Europe.

'Schneekäppchen' flowers are delicately bi-coloured, just like the beans.

'Schneekäppchen'

I'm not certain this bean is from southern Germany originally, I've searched, but can't find information about its origins. However I obtained it from Patrick Kaiser of Tatgut in Germany who is preserving regional varieties of beans. *Schneekäppchen* translates as little snow cap and is surely the same or closely related to the 'Snowcap' bean found in US catalogues. They are a wonderful half ivory and half coffee-coloured bean with maroon markings – looking like miniature snow crested mountains. It is said that these beans retain their rich colours after cooking, unlike many beans that lose their markings. They do keep a half pale, half darker colouring, but turn a brown, fudgey colour, very like cooked borlottis. They are kidney-bean shaped, much plumper and larger than most beans, and have a mild, earthy, flavour. Many say they have a texture similar to potatoes and can be used in place of potatoes in a meal. They are vigorous and productive, one of the shorter climbing beans and take only about 10-11 weeks from sowing to shelling.

CROATIA, BOSNIA AND SLOVENIA

In the former Eastern Bloc countries, traditions of small-scale farming and families growing for their own needs or to sell in local produce markets, have endured on a more widespread scale than other European countries. The regional varieties of beans are now being searched for and preserved. In Slovenia for example, the Agricultural Institute has collected and is storing more than a 1,000 samples of indigenous beans collected since the 1990s. The institute group some varieties under the name 'cherries' that are, as you might expect, quite small and round, with deep red colourings. The 'Crešnjevec' from Slovenia and the 'Domaći Cučak' from neighbouring Croatia would seem to be both cherry types.

'Domaći Čučak'

'Crešnjevec'

This has beautiful dark red, more oval than round beans that are speckled with white. The flowers are a beautiful pale purple and the pods are pale green, sometimes with bluish-purple flecks as they age. I find this germinates easily for me, and grows well. I like that the vines are not so tall as some, so the whole plant is easy to manage. Incidentally this bean is also listed as 'Cresijevec', but I think it should be 'Crešnjevec', the name of a village in Slovenia which is presumably where it originated.

'Domaći Čučak'

An old variety from Croatia, this bean is another wine red, cherry type, smallish with light speckles. Like 'Crešnjevec', it is robust, growing tall and is very productive. Both beans are delicate in taste. It's probably not worth growing both, so it would depend what seeds you can obtain. Čučak is a small town in Croatia, the home of this bean.

Phaseolus vulgaris 'Domaći Čučak': a climbing bean, it is very similar in appearance to the dwarf Dutch bean 'Reade Krobbe'.

'Bosnian Pole'

This bean – climbing of course – has the most amazing colourings and markings, which, to be honest, is why I am drawn to grow it. At first tan, covered with black stripes and swirls, it darkens to an unusual dark grey as it dries. A medium-sized, plump, round bean, it cooks well and holds its shape. It produces a flat romano-type pod, which is good to eat at the green stage, particularly if you like that rather different shape of green bean – so it's another useful 'all rounder' to grow. It seems happy in a cooler, British climate, producing a good crop.

Phaseolus vulgaris 'Bosnian Pole'. The bean dries to this striking dark grey colouring. When fresh the colouring is much less pronounced.

chapter 10

A basic guide to preparing and cooking dried beans

This is definitely a gardening book and not a cookery book. However growing, harvesting, drying, cooking and eating form one continuous, cyclical process and this chapter brings the cycle full-circle. In recent years the range of cookbooks offering wonderful recipes for beans has expanded considerably reflecting the growing interest in vegetarian and vegan diets. I recommend you turn to these books and I list some towards the end of the book (see p. 145).

My aim here is to explain some basics of preparation and cooking for two important reasons.

Firstly, if you associate eating beans with feelings of digestive discomfort, then you are unlikely to be very interested in growing them to eat, however delectable they are or however convincing the arguments of health and environment benefits. And secondly, while cooking dried beans may seem a simple matter of boiling them in water until they soften to be edible, that's only true up to a point. For that perfectly textured bean – holding its shape but pleasingly tender – cooking beans requires a bit of know-how and attention. So a short chapter on how to prepare and cook dried beans to avoid digestive difficulties and achieve that 'oh so perfectly' cooked bean seemed to be an essential addition to this book.

However, little did I realise what I was stumbling into. A great deal of lore and differing opinion circulates about how to prepare and cook dried beans. What one cook steadfastly recommends another may completely contradict. So after sifting through all the varying advice, here is what I have learnt. Keep in mind that there are a lot of 'it depends' – it depends on the variety of bean, its size, its age and how used you are to eating beans.

The root cause of any digestive problems is a type of carbohydrate in beans called oligosaccharides that our bodies lack an enzyme to digest. We rely on bacteria in our lower intestine to break these oligosaccharides down, producing gas in the process. The bacteria create different vitamins that are absorbed into the body as well as producing antibodies that help fight off certain types of infections. The bacteria also create an environment in the colon that lowers the risk for cancer. But while doing all their good work the bacteria release

Beans stored in tightly sealed jars and kept in a dry, cool, dark place.

gases, mainly hydrogen and carbon dioxide. These gases are odourless. The odour issue is quite separate from bean eating and results from sulphur-rich foods such as meat and eggs. So maintaining a low animal protein diet will reduce or could even eliminate any whiff.

People vary in how easily they digest beans, and some people may experience discomfort and some may not. Beans, too, vary in how digestible they are, because some have a higher proportion of the tricky carbohydrate than others. If you are not a regular pulse eater, then eat beans initially in very small quantities and build up consumption little by little. As your body gets used to eating beans, any problems usually disappear. Always remember though that a little bit of extra flatulence will be an indication that you're eating a healthy diet.

There are also several things you can do to assist good digestion. Shelled beans – either fresh or frozen – seem to be easier to digest than dried beans that have been resoaked. So one option is to focus mainly on producing beans to eat at the fresh or demi-sec stage, and freeze the surplus. And all beans must be cooked. Raw beans contain a toxin. In fact, the nutritional profile of beans is increased after they are cooked, contradicting the familiar idea that vegetables are more nutritious when eaten raw.

Soaking dried beans leaches out some of the troublesome carbohydrates, and so improves digestion. But soaking also removes vitamins, minerals and flavour. So some cooks suggest throwing away the soaking water, even changing it through the soaking process a couple of times, to assist digestion while others are adamant that beans should be cooked in their soaking water to retain maximum nutrients. My view is that making beans easy to digest takes precedence over preserving all the nutrients. There is little comfort in knowing you've ingested all the minerals and vitamins if you're suffering. So for maximum reduction of the indigestible carbohydrates opt for thorough soaking, throw away the soaking water and rinse thoroughly. Certainly if you are not used to eating a lot of beans, I suggest starting with this preparation regime. Fortunately no one disagrees over the most essential cooking process. The key to breaking down the carbohydrates into digestible sugars is long, slow cooking. The slow cook process may be simmering for a long time on the lowest heat or baking on a very low setting.

So far so simple you may think, but then it gets more complicated. For as well as preparing and cooking to aid digestion, the aim with cooking beans is to achieve the perfect texture so that they hold their shape but are creamily soft, not over- or under-cooked. So while, yes, it's a simple matter of simmering (or baking) them till they're done, there's a bit more of an art to it than that. Back to the soaking process.

SOAKING

The principle behind soaking dried beans is that it will soften the seed coat which both reduces the time needed for cooking while also, as I've said, leaching out some of the substances that increase windiness. However, small beans – black beans for example, or the smallest rice beans or even the 'Zolfino' with its thin skin – can be cooked without pre-soaking, and may even be better for it. Unsoaked they take longer to cook of course but you just cook them till they are soft. However, heftier dried beans will certainly need soaking first.

Soaking dried beans in plenty of water for several hours.

It not only depends on the type and size of bean, but also its age. Dried beans may be shelf-stable but they continue to dry out over time. Older beans will be tougher to cook. Here, by the way, is another good reason for growing and drying your own beans, because then you will know exactly how old they are. But as they age, they will certainly need soaking, perhaps for many hours to allow them to fully rehydrate. Remember too that beans may swell to twice their size when soaking so be sure to cover them with enough cold water so that they remain submerged.

Beans soaking in water should be kept at room temperature for at least 4-5 hours, and more if necessary. If you are soaking for more than 8 hours, overnight maybe, place the bowl in the refrigerator so that the beans don't start fermenting.

There is a quick-soak method if you don't have time for a long soak. Cover the beans with ample water and bring to a boil. Then remove and let them stand for an hour.

WHEN TO SALT?

There is much difference of opinion about when to add salt and whether adding salt at the wrong time makes the bean skins tougher, or not. To find the definitive answer I looked to the food science writer Harold McGee who says that salt in the soaking water will speed up the subsequent cooking time, but will not – contrary to common opinion – toughen the skins. Chefs also report that beans soaked in salted water cook up better, holding their shape and developing a more delicious, thoroughly seasoned flavour. So there is agreement that adding salt to the soaking water is a good idea.

Adding salt to the cooking water seems to make little difference except to the texture of the beans, producing a mealy texture rather than a creamy one. Most chefs seem to advise checking and adjusting seasoning when the beans are nearly or completely cooked.

'Gigantes'

An interesting study

... by Winham and Hutchins found that anticipation of flatulence after eating beans resulted in a perception of increased flatulence. They also found that if people had noticed increased flatulence, then after a few weeks of regular bean consumption, their flatulence levels returned to normal. They concluded that the long-term health benefits of eating beans are so great that dieticians should encourage people to put up with any temporary windiness, confident that it will decrease after a few weeks.

'Tresnjevac'

HOW LONG TO COOK?

There are substances in beans that need to be cooked to make them safe. The quantity of toxin varies considerably – kidney beans contain the most by far – but as a rule-of-thumb, the advice from heirloom bean grower and expert cook from the US, Steve Sando, is to boil all beans for at least 10 minutes at the start of the cooking time. The beans are still firm at this point and, he says, will survive a hard boil. Place the beans in a large saucepan or pot and cover with fresh water so that the water line is just above the beans.

Generous time baking in the oven or simmering on the lowest heat produces creamy and luscious beans and better digestion. Special lidded bean pots, typically terracotta, assist the slow, even oven-baking process. Slow cooking also allows the beans to absorb the flavours of oils, herbs and vegetables. The gentlest simmer in a big wide pot with plenty of water also ensures the beans cook evenly, and without being agitated too much so that they break up. Hard water containing minerals can reinforce the bean cell wall and therefore slow the

Freshly shelled 'North Holland Browns', cooked simply. They keep their caramel brown colour and are a starchy bean, so they split their skins but do not disintegrate.

softening of beans, so some suggest cooking in filtered water. Skim off any foam. With many beans there is the added bonus of the cooking liquid reducing down to a thick, flavoursome broth in which the beans can be served or added to other dishes.

Cooking your own, homegrown and dried beans, with only a little flavouring added, will reveal the true beany flavour and their heady aroma. Steve Sando explains how there is a moment in the cooking process when the beans are close to being ready that the scent from the added vegetables and herbs diminishes and the beans release their own special beany aroma.

Cooking times vary because it depends on the type of bean and its age. Beans may take an hour or three, and keeping an eye and testing regularly by popping one in your mouth to try is the only foolproof method (or squishing between finger and thumb). A cooked bean should be intact but collapse to a creamy pulp. Most importantly, make sure that the beans are well-cooked. Undercooked beans will certainly cause digestive problems. Beans will carry on cooking in their liquid, so either serve and eat, or drain to prevent overcooking.

WHAT TO ADD?

Add flavourings while the beans cook. This might be aromatic vegetables such as onion, garlic, celery, carrot or even fennel or leeks. And add herbs; rosemary, sage, thyme, bay leaf and savoury are good with most beans.

Kombu and garlic. Dried kombu seaweed can be added to beans as they soak and cook.

A warning about kidney beans

I don't grow kidney or cannellini beans myself for the simple reason that I don't like them much. However I should include the warning that dried kidney beans contain a toxin that can cause unpleasant symptoms (nausea, vomiting) if these beans are not cooked properly. Red kidney beans contain the most toxin, but white cannellini beans contain about a third as much. Soak the beans in water for at least 12 hours. You should always throw out the water that you've soaked kidney beans in before cooking them. Then the beans should be boiled for at least 10 minutes, ideally longer, at 100°C (212°F). This removes the toxin. Indeed, it's a useful rule of thumb to boil all dried beans for a good 10 minutes, just as a precaution. The beans are then simmered for as long as necessary to make them tender. The effect of the toxin is increased if the beans are softened without hard boiling so on no account cook kidney beans in a slow cooker (a lower temperature for a longer time).

Some suggest that spices added to the cooking pot help to make the beans more digestible as well as more delicious. It obviously depends on your recipe, but these include turmeric, nutmeg, cumin, ginger and asafoetida. Another suggestion is to soak and cook with kombu, a dried edible seaweed, because kombu contains an enzyme needed to break down the oligosaccharides.

Fresh herbs straight from the garden: sage, rosemary, savoury and bay.

However, three substances slow the softening of beans: acids, sugars and calcium. So wait if you want to add acidic ingredients such as lemon juice, vinegar, tomatoes or wine, or something like molasses (rich in sugar, calcium and somewhat acidic) until the beans are cooked through.

'Coco de Paimpol' cooked with garlic and herbs.

chapter 11

Sourcing
and saving seeds

Much of the fun – and the challenge – of growing beans is sourcing the special bean seeds that you want to grow. Hunting them down takes some perseverance and ingenuity. Most seed companies list a borlotto bean and perhaps a cannellino or flageolet as well, but very few go beyond what I consider to be one or two very basic beans. However all the 'must grow' beans I include in this book should be obtainable from specialist seed catalogues and small producers I will list at the end of this section. Many smaller companies offer certified organic seed, some focus on heirloom and heritage seed and on sustainable practices. Even so, these companies often sell only one or two shelling bean varieties, so be prepared to hop from catalogue to catalogue, ordering just single packets from each. However, it is important that we do support the suppliers of these 'one source' varieties, where their existence in the market is fragile, for otherwise they may disappear from the market completely.

Those readers who live in North America are lucky to be able to purchase from seed sellers with longer lists of beans. Some North American seed catalogues helpfully separate beans into bush (dwarf) beans dry and bush beans green – and likewise with pole (climbing) varieties. Until all seed companies cotton on and start listing their beans as 'dry' or 'green' then you have to read through the full list and rely on photos and descriptions to tell you if they are a variety suitable for shelling and drying.

With many of the harder to find bean seeds, there is likely to be only a few seeds per packet. So either order several varieties, buy more than one packet or expect to take a couple of years to save seed and build up the quantity so that you can have a bigger harvest.

It's also worth scouring online selling sites. Unfortunately there is no guarantee of the freshness of the seeds, although remember that bean seeds are viable for several years.

Vigilant bean enthusiasts will start finding beans on their travels. Make a beeline for local markets as these are the best hunting grounds, or even abandoned fields (or maybe not-so-abandoned fields. They didn't miss a pod or two, surely?).

The diversity of beans, as with all vegetables, largely disappeared in the 20th century with the emergence of commercially grown cultivars. Moreover across Europe traditional varieties of vegetables have been forced to the margins by EU rules. Fortunately, some people have been concerned at the disappearance of this living cultural heritage and have tried to preserve as many old bean varieties as possible. Gene banks and seed saving organisations have become crucial in the efforts to rediscover and propagate the many species of at-risk bean seed. In addition, committed enthusiasts have collected beans to propagate and preserve, or small-scale growers of distinctive regional beans have been supported to continue through cooperative schemes. And not just beans, of course, the same applies to all vegetable seeds. It is our work, too, as home gardeners – or as market gardeners and small-scale farmers – to sustain them as an essential link in the food system.

A WORD ABOUT NAMES

I obtained two different beans from a gardener in England who had brought them from her mother's garden in Slovakia. She told me that the beans had no names that she knew of, but one had been handed down through her family and the other had been bought in the local market in Slovakia. Only recently have we relied on commercial seed sellers and the reliability of named varieties. For centuries seeds were handed around among family and friends, bought in markets or travelled in the pockets of migrants and didn't need a fixed name.

The Slovakian beans, green and speckled, for that is what I now call them, will have other names, probably several. Beans are named by place (Lamon, Tolosa, Holland), by their colour (zolfino, black), their

Sourcing seeds from a wide range of companies.

markings (snowcap), their shape and size (rice bean, gigantes), taste (chestnut) and perhaps those who gave it (district nurse). They may even have quirky names linked to tales and traditions. One of the most memorable is the 'Turkey Craw' bean from the US, so named because it was apparently found in the craw of a wild turkey shot by a hunter. It should be said, however, that tales of seed found in the craw of a goose or turkey is a recurring theme in American horticultural folklore.

And so it is that names get lost, forgotten, changed and muddled up. With old bean varieties that are being collected and catalogued, there is, then, a problem with pinning down names. An added problem is that seedsmen often renamed vegetables to make them appear new and attractive to buyers. The result is that the same beans may turn up with different names or, vice versa, different beans turn up with the same names.

Official bodies have stepped in and tried to pin down the names and varieties, and approve those that can be sold commercially or grown in specific regions and conserved. If we buy beans that are officially listed we can be sure what kind of bean they refer to and what to expect if we grow it.

LANDRACES

During the last century, European agriculture, as with agriculture in other areas of the world, went through a significant change. Farmers and smallholders in the past would have selected and saved a proportion of bean seed from their crops at each harvest to cultivate in the next season. They would have selected from healthy, strong plants that had grown well on their land and that suited their needs. Over many years of selection the seed would have adapted to the local environment – its soil, fertility, availability of water, altitude, climate, resistance to local diseases – and served the food needs of the grower's family. Excess crops would have been sold or distributed among a local community. The farmers might have selected for particular characteristics, for example colour, taste, cropping early or hardiness. The crops were genetically variable because of repeated exposure to both natural and human selection processes. These crops are referred to as 'landraces' but are also known as 'farmer varieties', 'local' or 'traditional' varieties. Landrace beans are often referred to by their place of origin – 'Borlotto Lamon', 'Alubias Negras de Tolosa'. Local cuisine traditions evolved hand-in-hand with the beans, accentuating their cooking qualities and flavours.

Nowadays these genetically variable varieties have largely been replaced by genetically uniform, commercially bred cultivars. But genetic variability is a key to food security. Landrace crops are

Protected Designation of Origin

The European Union has awarded PDO – Protected Designation of Origin – to certain landrace beans, a badge that aims to recognise traditionally produced foods. The PDO badge helps to promote the preservation of the crop. Of course, if we grow a bean from Lamon or Tarbes in our home gardens, it no longer carries its PDO and the different soils and climate may slightly change the taste and character of the bean, but that is a small price to pay for growing these unique and flavoursome crops.

'Hagnauer Rote'

adaptable to a range of environmental pressures and so a crop may not be completely lost in one year. Landraces were not only maintained by farmers, they have been maintained in home gardens, allotments and market gardens. Some remain to this day, with growers keeping seed year upon year. Conserving landraces by seeking them out, growing them on, saving seed, is therefore important to ensure genetic diversity is not lost.

In Europe the loss of landrace and heritage seed diversity has been attributed to not only the shift to commercial farming methods but also to plant variety legislation and seed certification schemes. These are intended to ensure that seed meets the DUS (distinct, uniform and stable) criteria and has a registered, recognised name. But legislation has had the unintended consequence of drastically reducing the number of cultivars grown, often because of the associated costs of registration. In addition, seed providers have rationalised their seed lists, clearly preferring to retain popular varieties that are more likely to assure a profit, thus narrowing choice and variety even more.

HERITAGE AND HEIRLOOM

As the name suggests, heritage varieties – or heirloom as they are also termed – are old varieties that have stood the test of time and been handed down. The term heritage is not a precise classification and while some organisations, the Heritage Seed Library in the UK, for example, have attempted to pin down a definition, it remains a bit vague. Broadly speaking they are good enough varieties to be maintained by gardeners and small-scale vegetable growers. They are more stable than landraces, being found more widely and less tied to one locality. Heirloom, the term that is more commonly adopted in North America, has the added meaning of being handed down within families and this reflects the often strong personal links many have with heirloom beans.

It's important, however, that we don't revere heritage/heirloom beans just for the sake of it, as if the old varieties are automatically invested with some kind of superiority over modern cultivars. For sure, some varieties may have simply gone out of fashion, or been dropped from seed lists and deserve to be grown. But other varieties may have

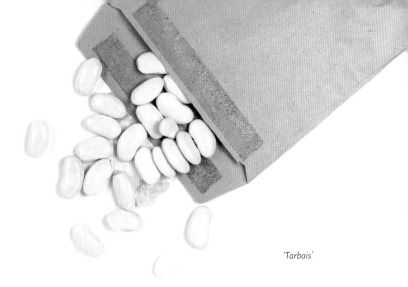

'Tarbais'

gone out of use for good reason, perhaps because they are not robust or have a low yield. Equally, more recently bred varieties may have advantages over older ones – I recommend some of the more recent flageolet beans for example.

OBTAINING HEIRLOOM AND HERITAGE SEED

In general, landraces, heirloom and heritage seeds are not nationally listed varieties, which means they cannot be bought on open seed markets. Seed that is not listed cannot be sold, but it can be swapped or gifted, or obtained through membership of a seed library or club. Sometimes those with seeds to offer get around this restriction by asking for a donation.

Why is it illegal to buy them? Firstly Plant Breeders' Rights ensured the economic viability of newly developed varieties of plants and provided the breeders with royalties on sales. Then in the 1970s European Union (EU) law made it illegal to sell seeds not registered on the National List or in the EU Common Catalogue, as a protection to prevent the sale of inferior and untested seed varieties.

SEED SAVING

So for hundreds of years smallholders and farmers kept seed from year to year. They passed it on, fathers and mothers to sons and daughters. Growers swapped with one another. The practice of seed saving had largely died out, although it is quietly increasing in many countries once more as many now question large-scale, centralised seed production. Seed savers are linked through formal and informal networks. Swaps might mean simply exchanging seeds with friends and family, in the age-old tradition, or participation in larger events such as Seedy Sundays (seed swap events that are held in many locations).

Preserving genetic diversity is essential because it is estimated that vegetable crops worldwide have lost 75% of their genetic diversity in the past 100 years. At the same time, there has been an increase in patented and genetically modified seed which is owned and controlled by a handful of companies. This control can't be applied to open-pollinated seed. Anyone can save their own seed. Campaigners aligning with several organisations are calling for seeds to be brought back into common and collective ownership and to give growers the right to breed and exchange open-pollinated seed.

Saving seed is not only easy (and cost-cutting of course) it enables us to gradually build up a bank of different varieties of beans that grow well in our own conditions and that we enjoy eating. You will be 'breeding' in effect, your own new, local variety. It will likely look and taste the same, but be imperceptibly adapted to your soil and climate. Moreover, we should not rely on the few growers who bulk up the heritage seeds on our behalf. If we want to maintain the diversity of seeds, seed saving needs to be part of every vegetable gardener's annual cycle.

With beans it's extremely easy to save seed for two reasons. Firstly *Phaseolus vulgaris* – the majority of beans you'll grow – will not cross with each other, or at least only cross very rarely. Secondly, the very process of growing and drying beans to store (see p. 49) is the same process as seed saving.

This still means it is sensible to grow individual varieties you want to keep for seed some distance apart from one another, but complete isolation is not essential. Two metres (6ft) apart will be enough, ideally

Open pollination

Open pollination occurs by insect, wind, bird, human hand or other natural mechanisms. Open-pollinated seed breeds true, so that the next year's plants will be roughly identical to its parents. This 'roughly' identical matters because the seed is not exactly uniform. An open pollinated plant will seem extremely similar to its parent plant but will not necessarily have the exact same genetic profile. It has the characteristics of the parent plants, but because there are no restrictions on the flow of pollen between individual plants, open-pollinated plants are more genetically diverse. This can result in some degree of variation within any one plant population, but this also allows plants to slowly adapt the growing conditions and climate on your patch of land, year-on-year.

Insect pollination. A garden rich in nectar-bearing flowers will also attract nocturnal pollinators such as this elephant hawk-moth.

4m (12–13ft). If you grow a lot of beans and don't have acres of space to ensure cross-pollination doesn't take place, you either risk saving seed from plants growing closer, or you isolate one or two varieties per year, relying on the fact that seed is viable (if stored well) for several years. When you pod the beans to dry and intend to save for seed, reject any that have an odd colouring or any other small defect.

It's a different issue with runner bean (*Phaseolus coccineus*) varieties however. These beans are pollinated by bees and cross with other varieties very easily (although not with other species of bean). So runner beans must be grown in isolation to be certain that the seed will grow true and that may even mean peering over the fence to see what beans the neighbours are growing. I have almost exclusively grown 'Gigantes' on my plot, and I have no close vegetable growing neighbours, so I can reuse the seed with confidence. (I also overwintered some tubers). If I want to grow the Polish 'Piękny Jaś' as an alternative – which is also a *coccineus* – I don't grow 'Gigantes' in the same year but save seed for the following year.

Just as with storing beans for cooking, those beans you want to save as seed should be kept in a cool, dry, dark place where there is little change in temperature. If you are aiming to save seed for some years, then storing in a cold place, even in a refrigerator, will preserve them.

chapter 12

Seed suppliers and further information

BEAN SEED SUPPLIERS

The following companies supply some bean seeds but in the case of most companies, they do not offer a wide selection.

United Kingdom

Beans and Herbs at the Herbary
www.beansandherbs.co.uk
Pippa Rosen runs this small organic seed company in Wiltshire and has the best and largest list of heritage beans in the UK. She is the true Queen of Beans and discovered the delights of heritage beans long before I did. The list also includes wonderful descriptions of the bean histories. A wide range of beans can be obtained through membership of the bean club. She has sourced some beans that were taken to the US and Canada by immigrants from Europe and have since been lost to their European country.

Chiltern seeds
www.chilternseeds.co.uk
This company supplies some unusual bean varieties.

Franchi, Seeds of Italy
www.seedsofitaly.com
Seeds of Italy offers a very good selection of Borlotti and other beans with Italian origins.

JungleSeeds
www.jungleseeds.co.uk
This company lists a number of traditional and unusual beans.

E.W. King & Co. Ltd and Suffolk Herbs
www.kingsseeds.com
King & Co. lists a dwarf cannellino bean and a borlotto bean.

Pennard Plants
www.pennardplants.com
Pennard Plants lists some heritage seeds and a small number of interesting, mainly European, climbing beans.

Real Seeds
www.realseeds.co.uk
This company lists what they describe as 'the most productive and tastiest beans they have been able to find' – a small, but good selection.

Thomas Etty Seeds
www.thomasetty.co.uk
With its quirky catalogue, Thomas Etty specialises in 'heritage, unusual and regional seeds' and offers a few distinctive and unusual bean seeds.

Garden Organic
www.gardenorganic.org.uk
Members of Garden Organic are able to purchase a range of seeds, including some beans. This is the home of the Heritage Seed Library, which requires an additional membership that gives members the opportunity to obtain a wide range of seeds grown by other members. The Heritage Seed Library (HSL) aims to conserve vegetable varieties that are not widely available. Once enough seed has accumulated, it becomes available for members to grow. The collection consists mainly of European varieties.

Seedy Sunday
https://seedysunday.org
Seedy Sunday runs seed swaps in many places in the UK. Finding heritage bean varieties may be pot luck but, particularly at the

larger events, you may be lucky. Some garden societies and regional environment groups organise seed swaps.

Hodmedod's British pulses and grains
https://hodmedods.co.uk
Hodmedod's is not a seed producer but an independent business founded in 2012 that sources and supplies pulses, including some beans, grown on British farms. They provide many different types of pulse for consumption. In 2020 they expanded their range to include some dried beans grown by two of their producers. These beans sold out almost instantly – testament to how popular beans are becoming. Since the beans have been produced organically, the seeds will germinate. So one option is to buy a pack of their beans, sow a few and eat the rest.

Europe

Association Kokopelli
www.kokopelli-seeds.com
This non-profit making organisation aims to promote the preservation of biodiversity through the distribution of organic and open-pollinated seeds of heirloom varieties of vegetables. It also aims to create a network of gardeners involved in seed saving and to help developing nations to develop sustainable organic agriculture. The association has branches in several countries, including England.

Seeds4All
www.seeds4all.eu
This platform provides links and information about 30 organisations, Europe-wide, that are concerned with preserving the diversity of seeds and to share information. This site provides web links to several seed suppliers.

'Black Tolosgao'

Austria

Arche Noah
www.arche-noah.at
This organisation preserves and cares for thousands of heirloom
vegetable varieties from German-speaking Europe and increasingly
from countries of Eastern Europe. Their seed list includes many beans.

Belgium

Belle Epoque Meise
https://belleepoquemeise.be
Guy Dirix is a bean collector who searches for lost varieties. He has
a selection of beans that he will supply for the cost of postage and a
small fee.

France

La Bonne Graine
www.labonnegraine.com
This seed company stocks several of the good French varieties.

Ferme de Sainte Marthe
www.fermedesaintemarthe.com
An organic seed producer with several old varieties.

Graines Baumaux
www.graines-baumaux.fr
This company stocks many French varieties.

Secret Seed Cartel
https://secretseedcartel.com
This is a small organic seed company based in southwest France
supplying unusual and heirloom seeds, including several difficult-to-
source beans.

'Merveille de France'

Germany

The Bean Atlas
www.bohnen-atlas.de
The Bean Atlas is a German site that collects and catalogues bean varieties and currently has over 3,000 varieties, with a priority on central European varieties. There are links to several more websites from this site, including a seed savers website. They send out bean seeds to growers to multiply and then return.

Deaflora
https://deaflora.de
This company has a seed list that includes many wonderful beans, several of them from northern Europe, including the Netherlands and Germany.

Project Bohnen Erhaltung (PBE)
https://projektbohnenerhaltung.jimdofree.com
This project, founded in 2011, is dedicated to the collection and preservation of biological diversity. The PBE owns the largest collection of old and rare beans in southwest Germany.

The PBE has set itself the goal of raising and widening awareness of old crops and, in particular, of their diversity. It wants to increase the importance of traditional varieties, to encourage people to grow traditional varieties and learn to appreciate the benefits of consuming them.

Tatgut
www.tatgut.de
This initiative was founded by Patrick Kaiser in 2020 and supplies heritage seed including an interesting list of beans; mainly old German regional varieties. The gardens are located in Tettnang, southern Germany.

Ireland

Irish seed savers
https://irishseedsavers.ie
The Irish Seed Savers Association conserve and distribute rare and heritage varieties and encourage the skills of seed saving.

Netherlands

De Tuinen van Weldadigheid
https://detuinenvanweldadigheid.nl
This organic seed producer has a large selection of beans – more than 150 varieties of beans are maintained and propagated in their gardens and sold in their online shop. The company combines the production of organic vegetables in its market garden with providing opportunities for people who require special care to work in the gardens.

Vreeken's Zaden
www.vreeken.nl
This seed company has a long list of beans, including many of the small colourful Dutch varieties.

United States

Baker Creek Heirloom Seeds
www.rareseeds.com
This company offers many varieties of beans.

The Bean Collector's Window
www.abeancollectorswindow.com
Russ Crow has been collecting beans since the mid 1970s and provides a catalogue of his beans, plus links to other North American sites. He tells an interesting story of his bean collecting in North America. He will give bean seeds to other growers and also has a network of growers who will grow particular varieties and then return a certain number of bean seeds.

Rancho Gordo
www.ranchogordo.com
Steve Sando is the founder of Rancho Gordo. He is a grower and enthusiastic and knowledgeable supplier of heirloom beans, many sourced from Mexico. The website is full of information, including Rancho Gordo books. Buy packs of beans, eat most and sow the rest.

Seed Savers Exchange, USA
www.seedsavers.org
Since 1975, the Seed Savers Exchange has grown, saved and shared
heirloom seeds, including heirloom beans, and led a movement to
protect biodiversity and preserve heirloom varieties. Their focus is on
preserving varieties of seed that gardeners brought to North America
when their families migrated and traditional varieties grown by
American Indians, Mennonites and the Amish. At the heart of the
organisation is a seed bank that houses a collection of some 5,000
varieties of beans preserved year to year in cold storage and grown out
periodically to refresh the genes.

Sustainable Mountain Agriculture Center Inc.
www.heirlooms.org
Bill Best has been collecting heirloom beans from the Appalachian
region for many years and has an extensive collection, offering many
for sale in his catalogue.

New Zealand

The Heritage Food Crops Research Trust
www.heritagefoodcrops.org.nz
The trust has a number of goals including sourcing, cultivating and
conserving a range of crops, particularly heritage ones and initiating
health research to explore the potential health benefits of these plants.
The Trust is currently attempting to find different varieties of heirloom
beans growing in New Zealand and a section of their website lists
several current varieties. Bean seeds are available to New Zealanders
in return for a donation.

'Groeninger Strogele'

INFORMATION

EAT is an Oslo based non-profit organisation with a global mission to transform our global food system through 'sound science, impatient disruption and novel partnerships'. EAT is focused on shifting the global food system toward a fair and sustainable model that promotes health for both people and planet. Cutting across sectors and disciplines, EAT brings together policy makers, industry leaders, researchers and civil society from around the world to develop realistic, practical solutions that yield big impact and fast.
www.eatforum.org

Slow Food is a global, grassroots movement with thousands of members around the world that links the pleasure of food with a commitment to community and the environment. It was founded in 1989 in Italy.
www.slowfood.org.uk

The Soil Association is a charity founded in 1946 that aims to transform the way we eat, farm and care for our natural world.
www.soilassociation.org

The Seed Co-operative provides open-pollinated seeds grown in the UK and although its range of beans is limited, the co-operative has an important mission to raise awareness about the vital role of the humble seed in building a resilient food system. The website includes links to other similar organisations.
https://seedcooperative.org.uk

Open Pollinated Seeds is an initiative to spread awareness about the importance of natural ways of propagation. It aims to highlight the fact that the availability of open-pollinated seeds for food production in Europe has been drastically reduced during the last 40 years.
http://open-pollinated-seeds.org.uk

The Bean Institute is owned by the Northarvest Bean Growers Association, a co-operative of dry bean growers in North Dakota and Minnesota. The website provides information on the nutrition and health benefits of beans, plus lots of recipes.
https://beaninstitute.com

COOKBOOKS

There are increasing numbers of cookbooks full of wonderful recipes for cooking beans, or pulses more generally – the following is intended to be a starter list.

Judith Barrett (2005). *Fagioli: The Bean Cuisine of Italy*. Pennsylvania: Rodale Press.

Georgeanne Brennan (2018). *French Beans: Exploring the Bean Cuisine of France*. Napa, CA: Rancho Gordo Press.

Jenny Chandler (2013). *Pulse: Truly Modern Recipes for Beans, Chickpeas and Lentils to Tempt Meat-eaters and Vegetarians Alike*. London: Pavilion Books.

Crescent Dragonwagon (2012). *Bean by Bean: A Cookbook*. New York: Workman Publishing Company.

Rose Elliot (2000). *The Bean Book*. London: HarperCollins Publishers.

Steve Sando and Julia Newberry (2017). *The Rancho Gordo Vegetarian Kitchen*. Napa, CA: Rancho Gordo Press.

Joe Yonan (2020). *Cool Beans. The Ultimate Guide to Cooking with the World's Most Versatile Plant-Based Protein*. New York: Ten Speed Press.

References and further reading

Albaba, K. (2007). *Beans: A History.* Oxford: Berg.

Berners-Lee, M., Hoolohan, C., Cammack H. and Hewitt, C.N. (2012). 'The relative greenhouse gas impacts of realistic dietary choices'. *Energy Policy.* 43: 184.

Berners-Lee, M., Kennelly, C., Watson, R. and Hewitt, C.N. (2018). 'Current global food production is sufficient to meet human nutritional needs in 2050 provided there is radical societal adaptation'. *Elementa: Science of the Anthropocene.* 6(1): 14.

Bliss, F.A. (1993). 'Utilizing the potential for increased nitrogen fixation in common bean'. *Plant and Soil,* 152: 157-160.

Calles, T., del Castello, R., Baratelli, M., Xipsiti, M. and Navarro, D.K. (2019). 'The International Year of Pulses – Final report'. Rome: Food and Agricultural Organization.

Carolan, M.S. (2013). *Reclaiming Food Security.* London: Routledge.

Didinger, C. and Thompson, H. (2020). 'Motivating pulse-centric eating patterns to benefit human and environmental well-being'. *Nutrients,* 12(11): 3500.

FAO (2015). 'International Year of Soils 2015. Healthy Soils for a Healthy Life'. Rome: Food and Agricultural Organization.

FAO (2016). 'Soils and Pulses: symbiosis for life'. Rome: Food and Agricultural Organization.

FAO, IFAD, UNICEF, WFP and WHO (2020). 'The State of Food Security and Nutrition in the World 2020. Transforming Food Systems for Affordable, Healthy Diets', Rome: Food and Agricultural Organization.

Genders, R. (1955). *Vegetables for the Epicure.* London: The Garden Book Club.

Havemeier, S., Erickson, J. and Slavin, J. (2017). 'Dietary guidance for pulses: the challenge and opportunity to be part of both the vegetable and protein food groups', *Annals of the New York Academy of Sciences,* 1392(1): 58-66.

Harwatt, H., Sabaté, J., Eshel, G., Soret, S. and Ripple, W. (2017). 'Substituting beans for beef as a contribution toward US climate change targets'. *Climatic Change,* 143(1-2): 1-10.

Kell, S., Maxted, N., Allender, C., Astley, D., Ford-Lloyd, B. and contributors (2009). 'Vegetable landrace inventory of England and Wales' retrieved from: http://randd.defra.gov.uk (18th April 2021).

Lang, T. (2020). *Feeding Britain: Our food problems and how to fix them.* London: Pelican Books.

Lang, T. and M. Heasman (2015). *Food Wars: The Global Battle for Mouths, Minds and Markets*: second edition. London: Earthscan.

Lappé, F. M. (1971). *Diet for a Small Planet*. New York: Ballantine Books.

Martens, G. von, (1869). *Die Gartenbohnen*, second edition. Reproduction produced 2012 by Nabu Press.

McGee, H. (2004). *McGee on Food and Cooking: An Encyclopedia of Kitchen Science, History and Culture* (revised and updated version). London: Hodder & Stoughton.

McSweeney, R. (2016). 'England's growing season now almost a month longer, says Met Office [online]'. *Carbon Brief Ltd*. Available from: www.carbonbrief.org [Accessed 29th January 2021].

Nazarea, V.D. (2005). *Heirloom Seeds and their Keepers: Marginality and Memory in the Conservation of Biological Diversity*. Tucson, AZ: University of Arizona Press.

Organ, J. (1960). *Rare Vegetables for Garden and Table*. London: Faber and Faber.

Rohde, E.S. (1943). *Uncommon Vegetables*. London and Aylesbury: Hazell, Watson and Viney Ltd.

Sando, S. (2011). *The Rancho Gordo Heirloom Bean Grower's Guide*. Portland, OR: Timber Press.

Scarborough, P., Appleby, P.N., Mizdrak, A. et al. (2014). 'Dietary greenhouse gas emissions of meat-eaters, fish-eaters, vegetarians and vegans in the UK'. *Climatic Change* 125: 179. [Accessed on 19th January 2018].

Spaliviero, G.P. (2015). *Libro dei fagioli d'Italia – Italia del Nord e Centrale Ricette e varietà*. [Kindle for iPhone] Amazon.com.

Spaliviero, G.P. (2015). *Libro dei fagioli d'Italia – Sud e Isole Ricette e varietà*. [Kindle for iPhone] Amazon.com.

Stickland, S. (1998). *Heritage Vegetables: The gardener's guide to cultivating diversity*. London: Gaia Books Limited.

Vilmorin-Andrieux, M.M. (1885, reprinted 1981). *The Vegetable Garden: Illustrations, Descriptions and culture of the Garden Vegetables of Cold and Temperate Climates*. English Edition published under the direction of W. Robinson. Berkeley, CA: Ten Speed Press.

Weaver, W. Woys, (2000). *100 Vegetables and Where They Came From*, New York, NY: Algonquin Books of Chapel Hill.

Winham, D.M. and Hutchins, A.M. (2011). 'Perceptions of Flatulence from bean consumption among adults in 3 feeding studies'. *Nutrition Journal*, 11:128-129.

Willett, W., Rockström, J., Loken, B., et al. (2019). 'Food in the Anthropocene: the EAT-Lancet Commission on healthy diets from sustainable food systems'. *Lancet*, 393: 447–92.

Wincott, A. (2020) *Growing Heritage: The Politics of Heritage Vegetables, Fruit and Seeds in Britain*. London: Routledge.

Index

Enjoyed this book?
You might also like these
from Permanent Publications

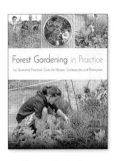
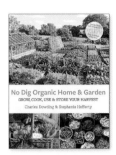

**Forest Gardening
in Practice**
Tomas Remiarz
£24.95
Step-by-step instructions
for creating your own
forest garden with 14
real-life examples from
Europe and the USA.

**No Dig Organic
Home & Garden**
Charles Dowding
& Stephanie Hafferty
£23.00
Learn how to create your
own no dig vegetable
garden and then preserve
and cook your harvests.

The Forager's Garden
Anna Locke
£9.95
How to create your own
edible sanctuary, for year
round food, in any sized
garden, with minimal
effort and care for
Nature too.

Our titles cover:
permaculture, home and garden, green building,
food and drink, sustainable technology,
woodlands, community, wellbeing and so much more

Available from all good bookshops and online
retailers, including the publisher's online shop:

https://shop.permaculture.co.uk

with 10% off the RRP on all books

Our books are also available via our American distributor, Chelsea Green:

www.chelseagreen.com/publisher/permanent-publications

Permanent Publications also publishes *Permaculture Magazine*

Enjoyed this book?
Why not subscribe
to our magazine

Available as print and digital subscriptions, all with
FREE digital access to our complete 29 years
of back issues, plus bonus content

Each issue of *Permaculture Magazine* is hand crafted,
sharing practical, innovative solutions, money saving
ideas and global perspectives from a grassroots
movement in over 150 countries

To subscribe visit:

 # www.permaculture.co.uk

or call 01730 776 582 (+44 1730 776 582)